Marketing Lessons from Food

Understanding Neolocalism and Its Business Implications

By Mohammad Zaripour

Copyright

© 2024 Mohammad Zaripour. All rights reserved.

No part of this book may be reproduced, distributed, or transmitted in any form or by any means, including photocopying, recording, or other electronic or mechanical methods, without the prior written permission of the publisher, except in the case of brief quotations embodied in critical reviews and certain other noncommercial uses permitted by copyright law.

Published by KDP Kindle Direct Publishing

About the Author

Mohammad Zaripour is a seasoned professional with a rich background in project management and engineering. His extensive experience is bolstered by prestigious certifications, including Project Management Professional (PMP), PMI Agile Certified Practitioner (PMI-ACP), Professional Scrum Master (PSM), and Engineer-in-Training (EIT). These credentials underscore his commitment to excellence and his continuous pursuit of knowledge.

With a career that spans multiple industries, Mohammad has expertly applied his project management and engineering skills to drive complex projects to successful completion. His approach combines meticulous planning, effective communication, and a focus on quality, drawing from both traditional and agile methodologies.

Author Notes

Ah, the author's notes—a chance for me to step out from behind the curtain and reveal a bit of the magic (or mischief) that went into crafting this book. Hi there! I'm Mohammad Zaripour, your humble guide through this marketing feast.

First off, a huge thank you for picking up this book. If you're reading this, you've braved the labyrinth of marketing jargon, survived the maze of business buzzwords, and are now about to embark on a delightful culinary journey of neolocalism and community charm. Kudos to you!

Now, let's be real: writing a book about marketing strategies while trying to avoid clichés and stay engaging is a bit like trying to cook a gourmet meal using only a toaster and a can of beans. It's challenging, it's messy, and yes, it involves a lot of experimentation. But like any good chef, I've tried to add a pinch of humor, a dash of local flavor, and a whole lot of heart to make it all come together.

In my spare time, I enjoy dreaming up quirky marketing ideas, supporting local causes, and occasionally pretending I'm a food critic (don't worry, my taste buds are fully trained). If you ever find yourself in Toronto, I might even invite you to a local café for a "pun-derful" coffee and a slice of "Mount Maple Pancake Stack."

So, here's to making your business unforgettable with a sprinkle of local charm and a generous helping of humor. May your marketing be as delightful as a perfectly crafted dessert, and may your community engagement be as warm as a freshly baked loaf of bread.

Happy reading, and remember—never underestimate the power of a good pun!

With gratitude and a chuckle,
Mohammad Zaripour

Table of content

Introduction 10

Chapter 1 14

Chapter 2 29

Chapter 3 43

Chapter 4 59

Chapter 5 75

Chapter 6 88

Chapter 7 100

Chapter 8 115

Chapter 9 129

Chapter 10 142

Conclusion 158

Appendix 164

Glossary 174

References 183

Abstract:

Ever wondered what your favorite local taco stand can teach you about marketing? Spoiler alert: It's more than just how to make a killer salsa. Neolocalism—the focus on local culture and identity—can turn your business into the hottest spot in town, just like that taco stand with the secret sauce.

Imagine this: Instead of serving the same bland, reheated marketing strategies as the big international food chains, you spice things up by incorporating local flavors. Your business becomes the talk of the town, and not just because of your questionable dance moves at the last community event.

By embracing neolocalism, you can create unique and authentic customer experiences that make people say, "Wow, this place really gets me!" It's like the difference between a microwaved burrito and a freshly made one from your neighborhood food truck. One is forgettable, the other is unforgettable (and might even come with a side of guac).

So, ditch the cookie-cutter approach and start thinking like your favorite local eatery. Who knows? You might just become the marketing equivalent of a five-star restaurant in a world full of fast food.

Introduction

Introduction

What Food Can Teach You About Marketing

Welcome, dear reader, to a culinary journey where marketing meets the magic of local flavors! Imagine this: you're at your favorite local taco stand, the one with the secret sauce that could probably solve world peace if given the chance. As you savor that first bite, you realize there's more to this taco than meets the eye. It's not just a delicious snack; it's a masterclass in marketing.

You see, while big international food chains are busy serving up the same bland, reheated strategies, your local taco stand is spicing things up with a dash of neolocalism. What's neolocalism, you ask? It's the art of embracing local culture and identity to create unique and authentic customer experiences. In other words, it's the secret sauce of successful marketing.

Now, you might be thinking, "What can a taco teach me about marketing?" Well, buckle up, because we're about to embark on a flavorful adventure that will leave you hungry for more (pun intended). We'll explore how businesses can build stronger connections with their communities by incorporating local elements into their marketing and operations. And we'll do it all with a side of humor, because let's face it, marketing can be a bit dry without a sprinkle of fun.

Throughout this book, we'll dive into the delicious details of neolocalism, from creating authentic local experiences to engaging with the community in meaningful ways. We'll share funny anecdotes, entertaining stories, and practical tips that you can apply to your own business. Whether you're a seasoned marketer or just someone who loves a good taco, there's something here for everyone.

So, grab a snack (preferably something local and tasty), sit back, and get ready to discover what food can teach you about marketing. Who knows? By the end of this book, you might just become the marketing equivalent of a five-star restaurant in a world full of fast food. And if nothing else, you'll have a few good laughs along the way.

Bon appétit!

Marketing Lessons from Food

Chapter 1

Chapter 1

The Flavor of Authentic Local Experiences

Welcome to the first course of our marketing feast! In this chapter, we're diving into the delicious world of authentic local experiences. Think of it as the appetizer that sets the stage for a memorable meal. Just like that unforgettable first bite of your favorite local dish, creating authentic local experiences can leave a lasting impression on your customers.

Let's start with the main ingredient: unique offerings. Imagine walking into a restaurant and being greeted with a menu that features dishes you've never heard of but can't wait to try. That's the magic of local flavor. Instead of serving the same old, reheated marketing strategies, why not spice things up with products or services that are unique to your area?

Take, for example, a local bakery that uses honey from a nearby apiary. Not only does it support local beekeepers, but it also gives customers a taste of something truly special. And let's be honest, who wouldn't want to brag about their honey-infused croissant on social media?

If you're running a retail store, consider stocking products made by local artisans. A clothing boutique might offer handmade scarves dyed with natural colors from local plants, while a bookstore could dedicate a section to books by local authors. These unique offerings not only attract tourists looking for souvenirs but also foster a sense of pride among local customers.

Restaurants and cafes can create seasonal menus that highlight locally sourced ingredients at their peak. For example, a summer menu might feature dishes with fresh berries from a local farm, while an autumn menu could highlight squash and pumpkins. This not only ensures freshness but also creates anticipation and excitement among regular customers who look forward to the new seasonal offerings.

Consider the power of incorporating local ingredients into your products. This not only supports local agriculture but also creates a unique selling point for your business. For instance, a brewery might use local fruits in its brews, or a restaurant could feature dishes made with locally foraged herbs. This commitment to local sourcing can differentiate your brand and build a strong connection with the community.

"Supporting local suppliers and using regional ingredients is not just good for business—it's good for the community." – Michael Pollan

Next, let's talk about ambiance. Creating an atmosphere that reflects the local culture and heritage is like setting the table for a feast. It's all about the details: local art on the walls, music from local bands, and decor that tells a story. Picture a coffee shop that doubles as a mini art gallery, showcasing pieces from local artists. Not only does it create a cozy and inviting space, but it also supports the local creative community.

Decorate your business space with local art and crafts. This not only beautifies your space but also provides a platform for local artists to showcase their work. Host monthly art exhibitions or craft fairs to draw in crowds and keep the atmosphere dynamic and engaging.

Marketing Lessons from Food

Organize events that celebrate local culture. A bookstore could host readings and signings with local authors, while a restaurant might hold cooking classes featuring traditional regional recipes. These events not only attract customers but also deepen their connection to your business through shared local pride.

Use decor that tells a story about the local area. A seaside café might decorate with vintage fishing gear, while a mountain lodge could use old skis and snowshoes. These elements make your space unique and memorable, creating a sense of place that customers will associate with your brand.

Creating a strong sense of place involves more than just decor. It includes how you make customers feel when they visit. Consider the overall experience you're providing—whether it's through the scents, sounds, or visual elements of your space. Every detail should contribute to a cohesive and immersive local experience.

"Ambiance is the silent ambassador of your brand. It speaks volumes about who you are and what you stand for." – Anonymous

Of course, no chapter on local experiences would be complete without a dash of humor. Imagine a restaurant that names its dishes after local landmarks or historical figures. How about a

"Mount Maple Pancake Stack" or a "Sir Syrup's Breakfast Platter"? Not only does it add a fun twist to the menu, but it also sparks conversations and creates memorable experiences.

Incorporate humor into your branding and marketing materials. A local brewery might name its beers after local legends or urban myths, while a pet store could have amusing signs like "Purritos: Your Cat's New Favorite Blanket." Humor makes your brand approachable and memorable, encouraging customers to share their experiences.

Share the history and cultural significance of your offerings in a light and entertaining way. A café could have a chalkboard with fun facts about the origin of its coffee beans, or a restaurant might print short, humorous anecdotes about local farmers on its menus. This not only educates customers but also makes their experience more engaging.

Add interactive elements that incorporate local culture. A bar could have a trivia night with questions about the local area, while a clothing store might set up a photo booth with props related to local landmarks. These activities create fun, memorable experiences that customers will associate with your brand.

Interactive experiences can significantly enhance customer engagement. Consider activities that encourage participation and interaction with your brand. This could include hands-on workshops, themed events, or interactive displays. The more involved customers are, the more likely they are to form lasting memories and emotional connections with your business.

"Humor and interactive elements are the secret ingredients that turn a good experience into a great one." – Anonymous

So, there you have it: the recipe for creating authentic local experiences that leave a lasting impression. By offering unique products, creating a local ambiance, and adding a touch of humor, you can turn your business into the talk of the town. And remember, just like a great meal, it's all about the details. Bon appétit!

Congratulations on completing this chapter!

You've taken another step towards mastering [chapter topic]. I hope the questions and answers have challenged you and sparked new insights. Remember, the goal is to not only understand these concepts but to see how they apply in real-world scenarios.

As you move forward, keep reflecting on how [chapter topic] influences your thoughts and actions. Take what you've learned and think about how you can integrate it into your daily life or business practices.

Stay curious, stay engaged, and don't hesitate to revisit these questions whenever you need a refresher. Learning is a journey, and every step counts.

Thank you for your dedication and enthusiasm. On to the next chapter!

How can your business uniquely reflect the local culture and heritage in a way that resonates with both locals and visitors?

To uniquely reflect the local culture and heritage, your business must first deeply understand and embrace the distinct characteristics that define your community. This involves more than just surface-level acknowledgments; it requires a genuine commitment to capturing the essence of local traditions, values, and stories. Start by exploring the historical and cultural narratives that have shaped your community. These narratives could include significant historical events, traditional crafts, folklore, and even the daily lives of local people.

Marketing Lessons from Food

For instance, if your business is situated in a town known for its artisanal crafts, consider incorporating elements of these crafts into your products or store design. Display locally made items prominently and share the stories behind them, whether it's a handwoven basket made using techniques passed down through generations or pottery crafted by a local artist. By showcasing these unique elements, you not only preserve local heritage but also educate your customers about the rich cultural tapestry of your area.

Creating an atmosphere that reflects local culture can also resonate deeply with both locals and visitors. The ambiance of your business should tell a story that aligns with the local setting. Use local materials in your decor—such as reclaimed wood from historic buildings or stones from nearby quarries. Play local music or host live performances by local musicians to immerse your customers in the regional soundscape. Incorporate visual art from local artists into your space, perhaps with rotating exhibits that keep the environment fresh and engaging.

To resonate with visitors, highlight what makes your area special and different from anywhere else. Offer unique experiences that they can't find back home. For example, a café could serve traditional regional dishes made with local ingredients, providing a taste of local cuisine that's both authentic and memorable. Host cultural events or workshops where visitors can learn about local traditions, from cooking classes that teach regional recipes to craft workshops led by local artisans.

Locals will appreciate your efforts to honor and preserve their heritage, fostering a sense of pride and loyalty. Visitors, on the other hand, will leave with a deeper appreciation for your community, having experienced something truly unique. By thoughtfully integrating local culture and heritage into every aspect of your business, you create an authentic and enriching experience that resonates on a profound level with everyone who walks through your doors.

What partnerships with local suppliers or artisans could enhance the authenticity and uniqueness of your offerings?

Collaborating with local suppliers and artisans is a powerful way to enhance the authenticity and uniqueness of your offerings, creating a distinctive identity for your business that sets it apart from competitors. Local partnerships bring a multitude of benefits, from ensuring high-quality, unique products to fostering a sense of community and sustainability.

Start by identifying the unique talents and resources within your local area. This might include local farmers, bakers, craftsmen, artists, and other small businesses that produce goods with a personal touch. For example, a restaurant might partner with local farms to source fresh, seasonal produce. This not only guarantees the freshness and quality of the ingredients but also supports the local economy and reduces the carbon footprint associated with long-distance transportation.

Artisans bring a wealth of creativity and tradition to the table. Partnering with local artisans to create exclusive products can significantly enhance your offerings. For instance, a boutique could collaborate with a local jewelry maker to design a line of custom pieces inspired by the area's history and natural beauty. These exclusive items would not only be unique to your store but also carry a story that customers can connect with, making their purchase more meaningful.

Additionally, featuring locally made products and services can create a strong sense of place within your business. For instance, a bookstore could sell locally published books or hold signings with local authors, while a coffee shop might serve pastries from a nearby bakery known for its traditional recipes. These partnerships showcase the talents of your community, providing customers with an authentic taste of local life.

To foster these partnerships, engage with your local community. Attend farmers' markets, craft fairs, and community events to meet potential partners and learn about their work. Building strong, personal relationships with local suppliers and artisans is key to successful collaboration. By understanding their stories and processes, you can better integrate their products into your offerings and communicate their value to your customers.

Local partnerships also enable you to offer a dynamic and evolving range of products. Seasonal collaborations with local suppliers ensure that your offerings stay fresh and relevant. For example, a bakery might feature a different local fruit each month in its pastries, keeping customers excited and engaged with new flavors and products.

Overall, collaborating with local suppliers and artisans adds a layer of authenticity to your business that mass-produced goods simply cannot replicate. It demonstrates a commitment to quality, sustainability, and community, enhancing the uniqueness of your offerings and building a loyal customer base that values and supports local craftsmanship.

In what ways can you incorporate seasonal and locally sourced ingredients or products to create a dynamic and ever-evolving customer experience?

Incorporating seasonal and locally sourced ingredients or products is an excellent strategy to create a dynamic and ever-evolving customer experience that keeps people coming back for more. This approach not only ensures freshness and quality but also adds an element of surprise and anticipation for your customers.

Start by aligning your offerings with the natural rhythm of the seasons. Seasonal menus, for instance, can highlight ingredients at their peak, offering dishes that are not only fresher and more flavorful but also varied throughout the year. In spring, your restaurant might feature dishes with tender asparagus and sweet strawberries from local farms, while in autumn, you could showcase hearty squash and crisp apples. This constant change keeps the dining experience exciting and ensures that customers always have something new to look forward to.

Beyond food, seasonal products can also enhance your retail offerings. A boutique could rotate its inventory to reflect the seasons, featuring light, airy clothing and accessories in the summer and cozy, warm items in the winter. This not only aligns with customers' changing needs and preferences but also creates a sense of novelty and exclusivity around your products.

To create an authentic and memorable experience, highlight the local origins of your ingredients or products. Educate your customers about the farms or artisans you work with, perhaps through stories on your menu, tags on your products, or posts on social media. This connection to the source adds value and meaning to the customer experience, fostering a deeper appreciation for what you offer.

Hosting seasonal events or workshops can also enhance the dynamic nature of your business. A café might hold a summer ice cream social featuring locally made flavors, while a craft store could offer holiday-themed workshops where customers create their own decorations using local materials. These events not only draw in customers but also build a sense of community and engagement around your brand.

Another effective strategy is to create limited-time products that capitalize on seasonal ingredients. Limited editions generate excitement and urgency, encouraging customers to visit your business before the opportunity passes. For example, a brewery might produce a special summer ale with local berries, or a bakery could offer pumpkin spice treats only during the fall. These seasonal specialties can become highly anticipated events on your business calendar.

Collaborating with local suppliers for seasonal products further enhances this approach. By using locally sourced ingredients, you ensure that your offerings are not only fresh but also support the local economy. This commitment to local sourcing can be a major selling point, attracting customers who value sustainability and community support.

Overall, incorporating seasonal and locally sourced ingredients or products keeps your business vibrant and responsive to the changing seasons. It creates a dynamic customer experience that evolves throughout the year, ensuring that your offerings remain fresh, exciting, and deeply connected to the local community. By embracing the bounty of each season and the talents of local suppliers, you can continuously engage your customers and build a loyal following that eagerly anticipates what you'll offer next.

Chapter 2

Chapter 2

Connection to Place

Welcome to the second course of our marketing feast! In this chapter, we're diving into the savory world of connecting your business to its place. Think of it as the main dish that brings all the flavors together. Just like a hearty stew that warms your soul, creating a strong connection to your local area can make your business feel like home to your customers.

Let's start with a pinch of history. Incorporating elements of local history and heritage into your business is like adding a secret ingredient to your

Marketing Lessons from Food

recipe. It gives your brand depth and character, making it more than just a place to buy stuff.

Imagine a bakery that names its pastries after local landmarks. How about a "Parliament Hill Pie" or a "Rideau Canal Croissant"? Not only does it add a fun twist to the menu, but it also sparks curiosity and conversations. Customers will love learning the stories behind the names, and it gives them a sense of pride in their local heritage.

Set up a corner of your shop with historical photos and artifacts related to your area. A restaurant could have a wall dedicated to old photographs of the town, or a bookstore might display vintage local newspapers. These displays create a sense of nostalgia and deepen customers' connection to your business.

Incorporate local historical references into your marketing materials. A café could print little-known historical facts on its coffee sleeves, or a boutique might share weekly posts about local history on social media. This not only educates customers but also positions your business as an integral part of the community.

Consider collaborating with local historians or cultural organizations to host events or create content that highlights local history. For instance, a wine shop could partner with a local historian to create a wine-tasting event featuring wines from historically significant vineyards. Such collaborations add credibility and enrich the experience for customers.

"History is the stage on which the story of your business is set. Embrace it, and your brand will resonate more deeply." – Anonymous

Next, let's add a dash of cultural significance. Highlighting cultural traditions and practices that are unique to your area is like seasoning your dish with the perfect blend of spices. It makes your business stand out and creates a deeper connection with your community.

Picture a restaurant that celebrates local festivals with special menus and decorations. During the Ottawa Tulip Festival, they could serve tulip-inspired dishes and decorate the place with vibrant tulip arrangements. It's a fun and festive way to engage with the community and show that your business is in tune with local traditions.

Partner with local artists and craftsmen to feature their work in your business. A coffee shop might use mugs made by a local potter, or a clothing store could sell accessories crafted by local jewelers. This not only supports local talent but also gives your products a unique story.

Host workshops and classes that teach customers about local traditions. A bakery might offer lessons on making traditional regional pastries, or a brewery could hold beer-tasting events featuring local brews. These activities provide hands-on experiences that deepen customers' connection to your brand and community.

Integrate local traditions into your everyday business practices. For example, a café could serve a traditional local breakfast on weekends or host regular cultural performances. This constant engagement with local culture helps reinforce your connection to the community.

"Culture is the soul of your community. Let it shine through every aspect of your business." – Anonymous

Of course, we can't forget the humor. Imagine a coffee shop that incorporates local slang into its menu. How about a "Double-Double Eh?" or a "Maple Syrup Mocha, Eh?" It adds a playful touch and makes customers smile. Plus, it's a great conversation starter and a way to bond over shared local quirks.

A local brewery could name its beers after famous local figures with a humorous twist. How about a "Sir John A. MacAle" or a "Laura Secord Stout"?

It's a fun way to pay homage to local history while keeping things light and entertaining.

Use playful and witty signs to catch customers' attention. A bookstore might have a sign that reads "Bookworms Welcome, Butterflies Optional," while a diner could have one that says "Bacon This Way, Happiness That Way." These small touches add personality to your business and make it more inviting.

Engage with your community on social media by incorporating humor and local culture. Run caption contests for local photos, share funny anecdotes about your town, or create memes that locals can relate to. This not only entertains but also builds a loyal online following.

Create humor-driven engagement opportunities by hosting fun local contests or challenges. For instance, you could organize a "Funniest Local Photo" contest and feature the winning entries in your marketing materials. Engaging with customers through humor strengthens their connection to your brand.

"Humor is the secret ingredient that makes a connection to place unforgettable." – Anonymous

So, there you have it: the recipe for creating a strong connection to your place. By incorporating historical references, highlighting cultural significance, and adding a sprinkle of humor, you can make your business feel like a beloved part of the community. And remember, just like a great meal, it's all about the flavors coming together in perfect harmony. Bon appétit!

Congratulations on completing this chapter!

You've taken another step towards mastering [chapter topic]. I hope the questions and answers have challenged you and sparked new insights. Remember, the goal is to not only understand these concepts but to see how they apply in real-world scenarios.

As you move forward, keep reflecting on how [chapter topic] influences your thoughts and actions. Take what you've learned and think about how you can integrate it into your daily life or business practices.

Stay curious, stay engaged, and don't hesitate to revisit these questions whenever you need a refresher. Learning is a journey, and every step counts.

Thank you for your dedication and enthusiasm. On to the next chapter!

How can your business authentically incorporate elements of local history and

heritage to create a deeper connection with your community?

Incorporating elements of local history and heritage into your business can create a profound connection with your community, fostering a sense of pride and belonging among your customers. Begin by delving into the unique historical aspects of your area. Research local legends, significant events, notable figures, and traditional crafts that have shaped your community. These elements can provide a rich tapestry of stories and symbols to weave into your business.

Consider how these historical aspects can be reflected in your business's story, decor, and events. For instance, if your town has a history of shipbuilding, you could decorate your space with nautical-themed elements, such as vintage ship models, maritime artifacts, and photographs of historic ships built in the area. These visual cues serve as a constant reminder of the local heritage and create a unique atmosphere that sets your business apart.

Incorporate local history into your brand narrative. Share the story of your business's connection to the community's past through your website, social media, and in-store materials. This could include anecdotes about your building's history, the origins of your products, or how your business honors local traditions. By doing so, you create a deeper, more meaningful context for your customers, enhancing their connection to your business.

Hosting events that celebrate local history and heritage can also foster community pride. Organize historical tours, lectures, or exhibitions that highlight significant local events or figures. Partner with local historians, museums, or cultural organizations to provide authentic and engaging content. These events not only educate and entertain your customers but also position your business as a community hub that values and promotes local heritage.

Additionally, consider offering products or services that pay homage to local history. A café might feature recipes inspired by historical local cuisine, while a boutique could sell handcrafted items made using traditional methods. These offerings not only differentiate your business but also preserve and celebrate the skills and traditions of your community.

By authentically incorporating elements of local history and heritage, you create a deeper connection with your community, fostering a sense of pride and belonging that resonates with both locals and visitors.

What cultural traditions or practices unique to your area can you highlight to differentiate your business and create a stronger local identity?

Highlighting cultural traditions and practices unique to your area can significantly differentiate your business and create a strong local identity that resonates deeply with your community. Begin by exploring the cultural richness of your area—celebrations, festivals, traditional crafts, culinary specialties, and local customs. These cultural elements can provide a distinctive flavor that sets your business apart.

Consider how you can integrate these cultural traditions into your products, services, and overall customer experience. For example, if your area is known for a particular festival, you could incorporate elements of that celebration into your business. A restaurant might create a special menu featuring traditional dishes served during the festival, while a retail store could stock items related to the festivities, such as decorations or traditional attire.

Hosting events that celebrate local cultural traditions can also enhance your business's local identity. Organize workshops, performances, or demonstrations that showcase these practices. For instance, if your area has a tradition of folk music, you could host regular live music events featuring local musicians. If traditional crafts are part of your cultural heritage, consider offering workshops where customers can learn these skills from local artisans.

Incorporating cultural traditions into your business's ambiance and decor can also create a unique and authentic atmosphere. Use local materials and design elements that reflect the cultural heritage of your area. For example, a café in a region known for its weaving traditions could decorate with locally made textiles, while a boutique might use traditional patterns and colors in its interior design.

Additionally, storytelling is a powerful way to highlight cultural traditions. Share the stories behind your products and services, explaining their cultural significance and how they connect to local practices. This not only educates your customers but also adds depth and meaning to their experience with your business.

By celebrating and highlighting cultural traditions unique to your area, you differentiate your business and create a stronger local identity. This approach not only attracts customers who value authenticity but also fosters a deeper connection with your community.

In what ways can you engage your customers in preserving and celebrating local culture and history through your business activities?

Engaging your customers in preserving and celebrating local culture and history can strengthen their connection to your business and the community, creating a sense of shared purpose and belonging. Consider interactive and participatory methods that involve your customers in meaningful ways.

One effective approach is to create opportunities for customers to learn about local culture and history. This could include hosting educational events, such as lectures, tours, or workshops led by local experts. For example, a bookstore could organize author talks focusing on local history, while a restaurant might offer cooking classes that teach traditional recipes and the stories behind them. These events provide an enriching experience that deepens customers' appreciation for local heritage.

Encourage customer participation in preserving local culture by offering hands-on activities. Partner with local artisans or cultural organizations to host craft workshops, where customers can learn traditional skills such as pottery, weaving, or painting. Not only do these activities provide a fun and engaging experience, but they also help keep local traditions alive.

Incorporate local culture into your products and services in a way that invites customer interaction. For instance, a café might feature a rotating menu of dishes inspired by different aspects of local history, encouraging customers to try new items and learn about their origins. A retail store could offer personalized items that reflect local culture, such as custom jewelry or artwork that incorporates traditional motifs.

Another powerful method is to involve customers in community events and initiatives that celebrate local culture. Sponsor or participate in local festivals, fairs, or parades, and invite your customers to join in. This not only showcases your commitment to the community but also provides a platform for customers to engage with local culture in a festive and communal setting.

You can also create opportunities for customers to contribute to the preservation of local culture. Launch initiatives such as a community history project, where customers can share their own stories, photos, and artifacts related to local history. Display these contributions in your business, creating a living museum that grows with community input. This participatory approach fosters a sense of ownership and pride among your customers.

Additionally, use digital platforms to engage customers in celebrating local culture. Create content that highlights local history, traditions, and events, and encourage customers to share their own experiences and stories on social media. This not only extends the reach of your efforts but also builds an online community centered around a shared appreciation for local heritage.

By engaging your customers in preserving and celebrating local culture and history through interactive and participatory methods, you create a deeper connection with your business and the community. This approach not only enhances the customer experience but also helps ensure that local traditions and stories are cherished and passed down for generations to come.

Chapter 3

Chapter 3

Unique and Personal Touches

Welcome to the third course of our marketing feast! In this chapter, we're diving into the delightful world of unique and personal touches. Think of it as the dessert that leaves a sweet and lasting impression. Just like a perfectly crafted dessert, adding unique and personal touches to your business can make your customers feel special and appreciated.

Let's start with the artisanal touch. Offering handmade or locally crafted items is like serving a dessert made from scratch with love. It showcases the skills and talents of local artisans and adds a unique flavor to your offerings.

Imagine a local bakery that sells handmade chocolates crafted by a local chocolatier. Each piece is a work of art, and customers can't wait to get their hands on them. It's not just about the taste; it's about the story behind each chocolate. And let's be honest, who doesn't love a good chocolate story?

Create exclusive product lines in collaboration with local artisans. A boutique might offer a limited edition of hand-knitted scarves made by a local weaver, or a coffee shop could sell custom-designed mugs by a local potter. These unique items not only attract customers but also create a sense of exclusivity and excitement.

Feature the process behind the products. A bakery could have a window into the kitchen where customers can watch the bakers at work, or a store might host live demonstrations by local artisans. This transparency not only highlights the craftsmanship but also engages customers and makes them feel part of the process.

Tell the stories of the artisans behind your products. For instance, a store could have profiles or interviews with the local creators whose products they sell, shared on social media or in-store displays. This not only enhances the product's appeal but also creates a personal connection between customers and the creators.

"Craftsmanship is the art of turning the ordinary into the extraordinary." – Anonymous

Next, let's talk about personalized service. Providing a level of customer service that reflects the local community's values and customs is like adding a personal touch to your dessert. It makes customers feel valued and appreciated, and it creates a memorable experience.

Picture a small café where the barista knows your name and your favorite order. They greet you with a smile and a friendly chat, making you feel like a regular even if it's your first visit. It's the kind of service that makes you want to come back again and again.

Train your staff to offer personalized recommendations based on customers' preferences. In a bookstore, staff could suggest books based on previous purchases or interests, while in a clothing store, they might recommend outfits that suit the customer's style and body type. This tailored approach shows that you care about each customer's individual needs.

Marketing Lessons from Food

Personalize your communication with customers. Send handwritten thank-you notes after purchases, or follow up with personalized emails offering special discounts or product suggestions. These small gestures can make a big difference in building customer loyalty and making them feel special.

Host special events or "customer appreciation days" where you invite loyal customers to experience exclusive previews or behind-the-scenes tours. This not only shows appreciation but also deepens the personal connection between your business and your customers.

"Personalization turns transactions into relationships." – Anonymous

Of course, we can't forget the humor. Imagine a restaurant that adds a playful twist to its service. How about a waiter who tells jokes while taking your order or a menu with funny descriptions for each dish? It's a fun way to create a relaxed and enjoyable atmosphere.

A local ice cream shop could name its flavors with a humorous twist. How about "Rocky Road to Success" or "Mint to Be"? It's a fun way to add personality to your offerings and make customers smile.

Encourage your staff to engage with customers in a fun and light-hearted manner. A barista could draw cute doodles on coffee cups, or a waiter might wear a funny hat on special occasions. These interactions create a joyful atmosphere and make the customer experience more enjoyable.

Run marketing campaigns that incorporate humor. A bakery might have a "Pun-derful Pastries" week with cleverly named treats, or a store could launch a social media challenge encouraging customers to share their funniest shopping experiences. Humor not only attracts attention but also fosters a sense of community and engagement.

Encourage customers to participate in humorous activities, such as submitting funny product name ideas or sharing their own quirky experiences. Feature their contributions in your marketing or on your social media, giving them a chance to be part of the fun.

"Humor is the secret ingredient that makes customer interactions memorable." – Anonymous

So, there you have it: the recipe for adding unique and personal touches to your business. By offering artisanal products, providing personalized service, and adding a sprinkle of humor, you can create a memorable and delightful experience for your customers. And remember, just like a great dessert, it's all about the love and care you put into it. Bon appétit!

Congratulations on completing this chapter!

You've taken another step towards mastering [chapter topic]. I hope the questions and answers have challenged you and sparked new insights. Remember, the goal is to not only understand these concepts but to see how they apply in real-world scenarios.

As you move forward, keep reflecting on how [chapter topic] influences your thoughts and actions. Take what you've learned and think about how you can integrate it into your daily life or business practices.

Stay curious, stay engaged, and don't hesitate to revisit these questions whenever you need a refresher. Learning is a journey, and every step counts.

Thank you for your dedication and enthusiasm. On to the next chapter!

How can your business incorporate artisanal products and personalized services to create a unique and memorable customer experience?

Incorporating artisanal products and personalized services into your business can create a distinctive and memorable customer experience that stands out in a competitive market. Begin by identifying the local artisans and craftsmen in your area who produce unique, high-quality goods. These individuals often bring a rich heritage and exceptional skill to their work, which can add significant value to your offerings.

Collaborating with local artisans allows you to offer products that tell a story, connecting customers to the community's cultural and artistic traditions. For example, a boutique might feature handcrafted jewelry made by local artisans, each piece accompanied by a card detailing the artist's background and the inspiration behind the design. This not only provides customers with a unique product but also enhances their emotional connection to your business.

Personalized services can further elevate the customer experience. Consider how you can tailor your interactions to make customers feel valued and appreciated. This might involve training your staff to remember regular customers' names and preferences, offering personalized recommendations, or providing custom options. For instance, a café could allow customers to create their own blend of coffee beans, while a clothing store might offer bespoke tailoring services.

Reflect on the small gestures that can make a big difference in customer satisfaction. Personalized thank-you notes, special discounts for loyal customers, or a complimentary service on their birthday can foster a sense of appreciation and loyalty. Training your staff to recognize and respond to individual customer preferences and needs is crucial. Encourage them to engage with customers, ask about their likes and dislikes, and use this information to provide a more tailored service.

In what ways can you enhance customer interactions to make them feel valued and appreciated, thereby fostering loyalty and repeat business?

Enhancing customer interactions to make them feel valued and appreciated is key to fostering loyalty and repeat business. Start by creating a warm and welcoming environment where customers feel comfortable and appreciated from the moment they walk in. Greet them with a smile, make eye contact, and offer assistance in a friendly manner.

Personalization is critical in making customers feel valued. Train your staff to remember regular customers' names and preferences. This can be as simple as recalling their favorite drink or asking about their last purchase. Such attention to detail shows customers that you care about their individual needs and experiences. Implementing a customer relationship management (CRM) system can help track these preferences and ensure consistent service.

Active listening is another vital component. Encourage your staff to listen attentively to customers, address their concerns promptly, and provide thoughtful responses. Showing empathy and understanding can turn a negative experience into a positive one, demonstrating that your business values its customers and is committed to their satisfaction.

Offering personalized services can also enhance customer interactions. Tailor your offerings to meet the unique needs and preferences of each customer. For example, a bookstore could provide personalized reading recommendations based on past purchases, or a spa might offer customized treatment plans. These personalized touches make customers feel special and valued.

Recognize and reward customer loyalty. Implement a loyalty program that offers exclusive benefits, such as discounts, special promotions, or early access to new products. Regularly show appreciation for your customers through personalized thank-you notes, surprise gifts, or invitations to special events. This fosters a sense of belonging and encourages repeat business.

How can humor and playful elements be integrated into your business to create a joyful and engaging atmosphere for your customers?

Integrating humor and playful elements into your business can create a joyful and engaging atmosphere that leaves a lasting impression on customers. Start by infusing your branding with a sense of fun and lightheartedness. Use witty and humorous language in your marketing materials, social media posts, and in-store signage. This can set a playful tone and make your business more approachable and memorable.

Consider hosting fun events that encourage customer participation and create a lively atmosphere. These could include themed parties, trivia nights, or interactive workshops. For example, a bakery might host a cupcake decorating contest, while a bookstore could organize a literary scavenger hunt. Such events not only entertain customers but also foster a sense of community and engagement.

Playful interactions can also be incorporated into your everyday customer service. Train your staff to use humor appropriately and engage with customers in a friendly, lighthearted manner. A well-timed joke or a playful comment can create a relaxed and enjoyable experience for customers. Encourage your team to have fun and show their personalities, as this can create a more authentic and engaging atmosphere.

Incorporate playful elements into your store's decor and layout. Use bright colors, whimsical designs, and fun props to create an inviting and cheerful environment. For example, a café might feature colorful murals, quirky furniture, or a playful chalkboard menu with humorous descriptions of the items. These visual elements can enhance the overall customer experience and make your business more memorable.

Hosting playful branding and lighthearted interactions can also extend to your digital presence. Share humorous content, such as funny videos, memes, or playful polls, on your social media channels. Engage with your followers in a fun and interactive way, responding to comments with humor and creativity. This not only entertains your audience but also builds a positive and relatable brand image.

By integrating humor and playful elements into your business, you create a joyful and engaging atmosphere that resonates with customers. This approach not only makes the customer experience more enjoyable but also helps your business stand out and encourages repeat visits.

How can your business incorporate artisanal products and personalized services to create a unique and memorable customer experience?

Incorporating artisanal products and personalized services into your business strategy can significantly enhance the customer experience, making it both unique and memorable. Start by identifying local artisans and craftsmen whose products align with your brand's values and aesthetic. These individuals often create high-quality, unique items that tell a story and offer a personal touch. For instance, a boutique might feature handcrafted jewelry or clothing made by local designers, each piece accompanied by a note about the creator and the inspiration behind their work. This approach not only supports local talent but also provides customers with products that have a meaningful story.

Personalized services can further elevate the customer experience. Consider offering tailored services that cater to individual customer preferences. For example, a café could provide customized drink options based on a customer's taste profile, or a bookstore might offer personalized book recommendations. These services make customers feel valued and appreciated, fostering a deeper connection with your business. Additionally, train your staff to recognize and respond to individual customer needs. Encourage them to remember regular customers' names and preferences, and to go the extra mile to make each interaction special. This could involve remembering a customer's favorite product, suggesting items based on their past purchases, or simply offering a warm and friendly greeting.

Small gestures can make a significant impact. Personalized thank-you notes, special discounts for loyal customers, or a complimentary service on their birthday can create a sense of appreciation and loyalty. These touches show customers that they are more than just a transaction; they are valued members of your community. By incorporating artisanal products and personalized services, your business can create a unique and memorable customer experience that fosters loyalty and encourages repeat business.

How can humor and playful elements be integrated into your business to create a joyful and engaging atmosphere for your customers?

Humor and playful elements can transform your business into a joyful and engaging place that customers love to visit. Start by infusing your branding with a sense of fun and lightheartedness.

Marketing Lessons from Food

Use witty and humorous language in your marketing materials, social media posts, and in-store signage. This can set a playful tone and make your business more approachable and memorable.

Consider hosting events that encourage customer participation and create a lively atmosphere. These could include themed parties, trivia nights, or interactive workshops. For example, a bakery might host a cupcake decorating contest, while a bookstore could organize a literary scavenger hunt. Such events not only entertain customers but also foster a sense of community and engagement. Playful interactions can also be incorporated into your everyday customer service. Train your staff to use humor appropriately and engage with customers in a friendly, lighthearted manner. A well-timed joke or a playful comment can create a relaxed and enjoyable experience for customers. Encourage your team to have fun and show their personalities, as this can create a more authentic and engaging atmosphere.

Incorporate playful elements into your store's decor and layout. Use bright colors, whimsical designs, and fun props to create an inviting and cheerful environment. For example, a café might feature colorful murals, quirky furniture, or a playful chalkboard menu with humorous descriptions of the items. These visual elements can enhance the overall customer experience and make your business more memorable.

Hosting playful branding and lighthearted interactions can also extend to your digital presence. Share humorous content, such as funny videos, memes, or playful polls, on your social media channels. Engage with your followers in a fun and interactive way, responding to comments with humor and creativity. This not only entertains your audience but also builds a positive and relatable brand image.

By integrating humor and playful elements into your business, you create a joyful and engaging atmosphere that resonates with customers. This approach not only makes the customer experience more enjoyable but also helps your business stand out and encourages repeat visits.

Chapter 4

Chapter 4

Community Engagement

Welcome to the fourth course of our marketing feast! In this chapter, we're diving into the hearty world of community engagement. Think of it as the side dishes that complement the main course, adding depth and richness to your meal. Just like a well-rounded meal, engaging with your community can make your business feel like an integral part of the local fabric.

Let's start with local partnerships. Collaborating with other local businesses, organizations, and charities is like adding a variety of side dishes to your meal. It creates a sense of unity and support within the community, making everyone feel like they're part of something bigger.

Imagine a local bakery teaming up with a nearby coffee shop to create a special breakfast combo. The bakery provides the pastries, and the coffee shop supplies the drinks. It's a win-win situation that benefits both businesses and delights customers. Plus, it's a great way to build relationships and support each other.

Plan joint events with local businesses. A bookstore could partner with a café for a book reading event, where attendees enjoy coffee and pastries while listening to an author read excerpts from their latest book. This not only drives traffic to both businesses but also fosters a sense of community.

Partner with local charities for fundraising events. A restaurant could host a charity dinner where a portion of the proceeds goes to a local cause. It shows that your business cares about the community and is willing to give back, which can build loyalty among customers.

Create programs that directly support local initiatives. For example, a grocery store could sponsor a community garden, or a gym could offer free fitness classes to local schools. These

Marketing Lessons from Food

initiatives demonstrate a commitment to the community and enhance your business's local reputation.

"Partnerships are the spice of local business success." – Anonymous

Next, let's talk about customer involvement. Encouraging customers to participate in community activities and providing opportunities for them to engage with your business is like inviting them to a potluck dinner. It creates a sense of belonging and makes them feel like they're part of the family.

Picture a restaurant that hosts monthly cooking classes where customers can learn to make their favorite dishes. Not only do they get to learn new skills, but they also get to connect with other food enthusiasts in the community. It's a fun and interactive way to build relationships and create lasting memories.

Create opportunities for customers to share their ideas and feedback. Hold regular panels or focus groups where customers can discuss what they love about your business and what could be improved. This not only helps you improve your offerings but also makes customers feel valued and heard.

Marketing Lessons from Food

Set up community boards in your store where customers can post about local events, share recommendations, or leave messages. It's a simple way to foster a sense of community and keep everyone informed about what's happening locally.

Engage customers in community-driven projects. For instance, a clothing store could invite customers to design a mural for their store, or a bookshop could hold a writing contest for local authors. These projects can create a sense of ownership and connection with your business.

"Involvement turns customers into community advocates." – Anonymous

Of course, we can't forget the humor. Imagine a local business that hosts quirky community events, like a "Chili Cook-Off" or a "Pie-Eating Contest." It's a fun way to bring people together and create a lively atmosphere. Plus, it's a great opportunity for some friendly competition and a lot of laughs.

Host themed events that incorporate humor and fun. A local brewery could have a "Bad Poetry Night" where customers read their worst poems for laughs, or a boutique could hold a "Worst Fashion Disaster" contest. These events not only entertain but also create memorable experiences for attendees.

Marketing Lessons from Food

Run social media challenges with a humorous twist. A café might launch a "Latte Art Fail" challenge where customers post their funniest attempts at latte art. The best (or worst) entries could win a prize, generating engagement and laughs online.

Use humor in your decor and signage. A bar might have funny quotes or jokes written on chalkboards, or a retail store could have amusing fitting room signs. These small touches can create a welcoming and light-hearted environment that customers enjoy.

Organize "Fun Days" where humor and local culture intersect. For instance, a local market could have a "Funky Fruit Festival" featuring quirky fruit-related activities and games. These events can bring the community together in a playful and engaging way.

"Humor is the glue that holds communities together." – Anonymous

So, there you have it: the recipe for engaging with your community. By forming local partnerships, involving customers in activities, and adding a sprinkle of humor, you can create a sense of unity and belonging that makes your business feel like a cherished part of the community. And remember, just like a great meal, it's all about the love and care you put into it. Bon appétit!

Congratulations on completing this chapter!

You've taken another step towards mastering [chapter topic]. I hope the questions and answers have challenged you and sparked new insights. Remember, the goal is to not only understand these concepts but to see how they apply in real-world scenarios.

As you move forward, keep reflecting on how [chapter topic] influences your thoughts and actions. Take what you've learned and think about how you can integrate it into your daily life or business practices.

Stay curious, stay engaged, and don't hesitate to revisit these questions whenever you need a refresher. Learning is a journey, and every step counts.

Thank you for your dedication and enthusiasm. On to the next chapter!

How can your business form meaningful partnerships with local organizations and other businesses to create a stronger sense of community?

Forming meaningful partnerships with local organizations and other businesses is a strategic approach to create a stronger sense of community and enhance your business's local presence. Start by identifying organizations and businesses that share similar values and goals. These could be local charities, schools, non-profits, or other businesses that complement your services or products. For instance, a café might partner with a local bakery to offer co-branded products, or a bookstore might collaborate with a nearby school to host reading events.

Partnerships can be mutually beneficial, enhancing community presence and contributing to local causes. For example, a retail store could partner with a local non-profit to host a charity event, where a portion of the sales is donated to the non-profit's cause. This not only supports the local organization but also attracts customers who are passionate about giving back to their community. Additionally, these partnerships can provide opportunities for cross-promotion, where both parties benefit from increased visibility and customer engagement.

To ensure these partnerships are meaningful, focus on building long-term relationships rather than one-off collaborations. Regularly engage with your partners, seek their input on community initiatives, and find ways to support each other's goals. This could involve joint marketing campaigns, co-hosted events, or collaborative community projects. By working together, you can create a network of support that strengthens the community and enhances your business's reputation as a committed and engaged local entity.

In what ways can you involve your customers in community activities and initiatives to foster a sense of belonging and loyalty?

Involving your customers in community activities and initiatives is a powerful way to foster a sense of belonging and loyalty. Start by creating interactive and participatory methods that encourage customer engagement. This could involve organizing community events, such as local clean-up drives, charity runs, or cultural festivals, where customers can actively participate and contribute. For instance, a gym might organize a charity fitness challenge, encouraging members to raise funds for a local cause while participating in a fun and healthy activity.

Create opportunities for customers to contribute to community projects through your business. This could involve setting up donation stations in your store, where customers can donate items for local charities, or organizing volunteer days where customers and employees work together on community projects. Additionally, you can offer incentives for customer participation, such as discounts, loyalty points, or recognition in your store or on social media.

Engaging customers in community initiatives also involves effective communication. Use your marketing channels, such as social media, newsletters, and in-store signage, to inform customers about upcoming events and initiatives. Share stories and updates about the impact of their contributions, highlighting how their involvement is making a difference in the community. This not only keeps customers informed but also reinforces their sense of belonging and pride in supporting local causes.

By involving your customers in community activities and initiatives, you create a sense of unity and shared purpose. This fosters loyalty, as customers feel connected to your business and the community, encouraging repeat visits and positive word-of-mouth recommendations.

How can humor and fun be incorporated into your community engagement efforts to make them more enjoyable and memorable for participants?

Incorporating humor and fun into your community engagement efforts can make them more enjoyable and memorable for participants, fostering a positive and vibrant community atmosphere. Start by organizing playful events that encourage participation and laughter. This could involve hosting themed parties, talent shows, or friendly competitions. For example, a pet store might organize a costume contest for pets, while a restaurant could host a food-eating challenge. These events not only entertain but also bring people together in a fun and relaxed environment.

Use lighthearted promotions and fun activities to engage your community. This could involve creating humorous social media campaigns, such as a meme contest or a funny photo challenge, where participants can share their entries online. Additionally, consider organizing scavenger hunts, trivia nights, or game tournaments that encourage teamwork and friendly competition. For instance, a bookstore might host a literary trivia night, while a bar could organize a karaoke competition. These activities not only engage participants but also create lasting memories and positive associations with your business.

Humor can also be integrated into your everyday interactions with the community. Train your staff to use humor appropriately in their customer interactions, creating a friendly and approachable atmosphere. Encourage them to share lighthearted stories, jokes, or playful comments that make customers smile. Additionally, incorporate playful elements into your store's decor and branding, such as funny signs, quirky displays, or amusing product descriptions. These touches can make your business more inviting and memorable.

By incorporating humor and fun into your community engagement efforts, you create a joyful and engaging atmosphere that resonates with participants. This approach not only enhances the community experience but also strengthens the connection between your business and the community, fostering loyalty and positive word-of-mouth recommendations.

How can your business form meaningful partnerships with local organizations and other businesses to create a stronger sense of community?

Forming meaningful partnerships with local organizations and businesses is essential for fostering a strong sense of community and enhancing your business's local presence. Start by identifying potential collaborators whose values and objectives align with yours. These could include non-profits, local schools, charities, or other businesses that offer complementary

Marketing Lessons from Food

services. For instance, a bookstore could partner with a local café to host book readings and coffee tastings, creating a mutually beneficial event that draws in customers from both businesses.

Such partnerships can amplify your community presence and contribute to local causes. Consider joint initiatives that address community needs, like a retail store partnering with a local food bank for a donation drive, or a gym collaborating with a health organization to host wellness workshops. These collaborations not only support community causes but also showcase your business's commitment to social responsibility.

To cultivate lasting partnerships, focus on building long-term relationships. Engage regularly with your partners, participate in their events, and support their initiatives. This could involve co-sponsoring local festivals, collaborating on marketing campaigns, or joining forces for community improvement projects. By working closely with local organizations and businesses, you create a network of support that strengthens the community and enhances your business's reputation as a dedicated local entity.

In what ways can you involve your customers in community activities and initiatives to foster a sense of belonging and loyalty?

Involving your customers in community activities and initiatives is crucial for fostering a sense of belonging and loyalty. Start by organizing interactive and participatory events that encourage customer engagement. Examples include local charity runs, community clean-up days, or cultural festivals where customers can actively contribute. For instance, a coffee shop could organize a community clean-up followed by a coffee social, encouraging customers to bond over a shared cause.

Creating opportunities for customer involvement also involves setting up platforms where they can contribute to community projects through your business. This might include donation drives, volunteer sign-up stations, or community boards where customers can post ideas and suggestions. Offering incentives such as discounts, loyalty points, or special recognition can further motivate participation.

Effective communication is key to involving customers in community initiatives. Use your marketing channels to inform customers about upcoming events and initiatives, and share stories of how their contributions are making a difference. Highlighting these impacts can reinforce their sense of belonging and pride in supporting local causes.

By involving customers in community activities and initiatives, you create a shared sense of purpose and unity. This not only fosters loyalty but also encourages repeat visits and positive word-of-mouth, as customers feel a deeper connection to your business and the community.

How can humor and fun be incorporated into your community engagement efforts to make them more enjoyable and memorable for participants?

Incorporating humor and fun into your community engagement efforts can make them more enjoyable and memorable, fostering a positive and vibrant community atmosphere. Start by organizing playful events that encourage participation and laughter. This could involve hosting themed parties, talent shows, or friendly competitions. For example, a pet store might organize a costume contest for pets, while a restaurant could host a food-eating challenge. These events not only entertain but also bring people together in a fun and relaxed environment.

Use lighthearted promotions and fun activities to engage your community. This could involve creating humorous social media campaigns, such as a meme contest or a funny photo challenge, where participants can share their entries online. Additionally, consider organizing scavenger hunts, trivia nights, or game tournaments that encourage teamwork and friendly competition. For instance, a bookstore might host a literary trivia night, while a bar could organize a karaoke competition. These activities not only engage participants but also create lasting memories and positive associations with your business.

Humor can also be integrated into your everyday interactions with the community. Train your staff to use humor appropriately in their customer interactions, creating a friendly and approachable atmosphere. Encourage them to share lighthearted stories, jokes, or playful comments that make customers smile. Additionally, incorporate playful elements into your store's decor and branding, such as funny signs, quirky displays, or amusing product descriptions. These touches can make your business more inviting and memorable.

By incorporating humor and fun into your community engagement efforts, you create a joyful and engaging atmosphere that resonates with participants. This approach not only enhances the community experience but also strengthens the connection between your business and the community, fostering loyalty and positive word-of-mouth recommendations.

Chapter 5

Chapter 5

Cultural and Place-Based Narratives

Welcome to the fifth course of our marketing feast! In this chapter, we're diving into the rich and flavorful world of cultural and place-based narratives. Think of it as the storytelling that brings your meal to life, adding depth and meaning to every bite. Just like a great story, weaving cultural and place-based narratives into your business can create a deep connection with your customers.

Let's start with the art of storytelling. Using storytelling to convey the history, culture, and values of your local area is like adding a captivating plot to your meal. It makes your business more engaging and memorable, turning a simple transaction into an experience.

Imagine a local café that shares the story of its founding on its menu. The owners could tell the tale of how they started the café with a single espresso machine and a dream, highlighting the challenges and triumphs along the way. Customers love a good origin story, and it makes them feel more connected to the business.

Feature stories from your customers about their experiences with your business. A bookstore could have a section on its website where readers share how a particular book changed their life. These narratives create a sense of community and show that your business values its customers' voices.

Incorporate interesting historical facts about your location into your marketing. A brewery could have fun facts about the history of brewing in the area on its beer labels or in its taproom. These stories add depth to your brand and provide engaging talking points for customers.

Understanding the power of storytelling in marketing involves delving into the psychological impact stories have on people. Studies show that narratives are easier to remember than facts alone because they evoke emotions and create personal connections. This can be particularly potent when tied to a local context, as it leverages shared cultural and historical touchpoints.

"People think that stories are shaped by people. In fact, it's the other way around." – Terry Pratchett

Next, let's talk about local imagery. Utilizing images and symbols that are representative of your local area in branding and advertising is like adding visual flair to your meal. It makes your business instantly recognizable and creates a sense of place.

Picture a brewery that uses local landmarks in its branding. Each beer label features a different iconic spot in the city, from the historic downtown clock tower to the scenic riverfront. It's a fun way to celebrate the local area and make customers feel a sense of pride in their community.

Collaborate with local artists to create unique artwork for your business. A restaurant could feature murals painted by local artists that depict scenes from the community. This not only beautifies your space but also supports local talent.

Incorporate cultural symbols into your products and marketing materials. A bakery might use traditional patterns from local indigenous tribes in their packaging design. This honors local culture and adds a unique visual element to your brand.

While local imagery can be a powerful tool, it's important to be mindful of its use. Misappropriation of cultural symbols can lead to backlash and alienate the very community you're trying to engage. Always ensure that the use of local imagery is respectful and appropriate, and consider involving community members in the design process.

Include diagrams or charts that illustrate the impact of using local imagery in marketing. For instance, a chart could show the increase in customer engagement and brand recognition after a business incorporated local artwork into its branding.

Of course, we can't forget the humor. Imagine a restaurant that incorporates local legends and folklore into its marketing. How about a burger named after a famous local ghost or a cocktail inspired by a legendary local hero? It's a playful way to add personality to your offerings and make customers smile.

And let's not forget the power of a good pun. A local bakery could create a series of pastries named after local puns. How about "Ottawa-waffles" or

"Maple Leaf Macarons"? It's a fun way to engage with customers and showcase your business's creativity.

Host events that play on local legends or humorous aspects of your community. A café could have a "Local Lore Latte" night where customers share their favorite local ghost stories over coffee. It's a great way to create a lively atmosphere and draw in crowds.

Use humor in your signage and advertisements. A local diner could have funny sayings or jokes on their chalkboard menu. It's a simple way to add personality to your business and make customers smile as soon as they walk in.

Share anecdotes about how humor has positively impacted your business. For example, a restaurant owner might recount how a funny sign about a local event brought in a flood of customers who appreciated the lighthearted approach.

Pose questions to your readers to encourage deeper thought about the topic. For example:

- How can your business incorporate local narratives without seeming forced or inauthentic?

- What are some unique aspects of your local culture that you could highlight in your marketing?

Encourage your readers to hold a workshop with their team to brainstorm ways to incorporate local stories into their marketing. Provide prompts such as:

- Identify three local legends or historical events that could be woven into your business's story.
- Create a draft of a social media post that uses local imagery and humor.

Have readers create a visual storyboard that maps out how they will use local imagery in their branding. This can include sketches, photos, or digital designs that represent their vision.

So, there you have it: the recipe for weaving cultural and place-based narratives into your business. By using storytelling, incorporating local imagery, and adding a sprinkle of humor, you can create a deep and meaningful connection with your customers. And remember, just like a great story, it's all about the details that bring it to life. Bon appétit!

Congratulations on completing this chapter!

You've taken another step towards mastering [chapter topic]. I hope the questions and answers have challenged you and sparked new insights. Remember, the goal is to not only understand these concepts but to see how they apply in real-world scenarios.

As you move forward, keep reflecting on how [chapter topic] influences your thoughts and actions. Take what you've learned and think about how you can integrate it into your daily life or business practices.

Stay curious, stay engaged, and don't hesitate to revisit these questions whenever you need a refresher. Learning is a journey, and every step counts.

Thank you for your dedication and enthusiasm. On to the next chapter!

How can your business incorporate local narratives without seeming forced or inauthentic?

Incorporating local narratives into your business requires a delicate balance to ensure authenticity and avoid seeming forced. The key is to deeply understand and genuinely connect with the local culture. Start by immersing yourself in the local

Marketing Lessons from Food

community—attend events, engage with residents, and learn about the area's history and traditions. This firsthand experience will provide a wealth of authentic stories and insights that you can weave into your business narrative.

When incorporating these narratives, focus on natural integration rather than overt or superficial mentions. For example, if your business is a café in a historic town, you might highlight how your building played a role in a significant local event or how your recipes are inspired by traditional local cuisine. Share these stories in a way that feels organic, perhaps through casual conversations with customers, informative placards, or engaging blog posts.

Authenticity also comes from involving the community in your storytelling. Feature real stories from local residents, invite local historians to share their knowledge, or collaborate with local artists to create displays that reflect the area's heritage. This approach not only lends credibility but also fosters a sense of pride and ownership among the community.

Moreover, ensure that your staff is knowledgeable about these narratives and can share them confidently with customers. Training your team to understand and appreciate local history and culture will enable them to convey these stories authentically, enhancing the overall customer experience.

By deeply engaging with the local culture and naturally integrating its narratives into your business, you create a genuine and meaningful connection with both locals and visitors, enriching their experience and strengthening your community ties.

What are some unique aspects of your local culture that you could highlight in your marketing?

Highlighting unique aspects of your local culture in your marketing can set your business apart and create a strong connection with your audience. Start by identifying the distinctive elements of your local culture—these could be historical landmarks, traditional festivals, culinary specialties, or unique crafts. For instance, if your area is known for its vibrant music scene, you could incorporate local music into your marketing campaigns, host live performances, or feature local musicians in your advertisements.

Cultural festivals and events provide rich material for marketing. If your community celebrates a particular festival, consider how your business can participate and promote this event. You could create special offers, themed products, or social media campaigns that tie into the festival's theme. Sharing stories and images from these events can showcase your business's connection to local traditions and attract customers who are interested in the cultural experience.

Local cuisine is another powerful way to highlight culture. Feature traditional dishes or locally sourced ingredients in your menu or products, and share the stories behind them. For example, a restaurant might promote a dish that's a local favorite, explaining its history and significance in the community. This not only appeals to locals who cherish these traditions but also attracts visitors looking for an authentic experience.

Engaging local personalities and influencers can also amplify your marketing efforts. Collaborate with well-known local figures, whether they are artists, chefs, or historians, to co-create content or events that celebrate your area's unique culture. Their endorsement and participation can lend authenticity and broaden your reach.

By thoughtfully highlighting the unique aspects of your local culture in your marketing, you create a compelling narrative that resonates with both locals and visitors, fostering a sense of pride and belonging while attracting new customers.

Encouraging Workshops and Brainstorming Sessions

Encouraging your readers to hold workshops with their team can be a highly effective way to generate creative ideas for incorporating local stories into their marketing. Workshops provide a collaborative environment where diverse perspectives can spark innovative concepts. Here's how you can guide your readers to facilitate these sessions:

Identify three local legends or historical events that could be woven into your business's story. Begin by researching local legends or significant historical events that are not only fascinating but also relevant to your business. During the workshop, encourage team members to share their favorite local stories and discuss how these narratives could be integrated into your brand. For instance, a boutique hotel might uncover a story about a famous artist who once stayed in the area, inspiring a themed suite or an art exhibit within the hotel.

Create a draft of a social media post that uses local imagery and humor. Social media is a powerful tool for storytelling. Challenge your team to draft social media posts that incorporate local landmarks, cultural references, or humorous anecdotes. For example, a bakery could post a fun, light-hearted story about a famous local figure who supposedly loved a particular type of pastry they sell. Encourage the use of local dialects or slang to add authenticity and humor. This exercise not only helps in creating engaging content but also in understanding how local culture can be presented in a relatable and entertaining manner.

By conducting these workshops, your readers can harness the collective creativity of their team to develop authentic and engaging marketing strategies that highlight local culture. This approach not only enriches their brand's narrative but also strengthens their connection with the community, making their business a memorable part of the local landscape.

Chapter 6

Chapter 6

Environmental Sustainability

Welcome to the sixth course of our marketing feast! In this chapter, we're diving into the refreshing world of environmental sustainability. Think of it as the palate cleanser that leaves you feeling good about your choices. Just like a refreshing sorbet, implementing environmentally sustainable practices can make your business stand out and leave a positive impact on your community.

Let's start with eco-friendly practices. Implementing environmentally sustainable practices is like choosing organic ingredients for your meal. It shows that you care about the quality of your offerings and the well-being of your customers and the planet.

Imagine a local café that uses compostable cups and utensils, sources its ingredients from local organic farms, and has a robust recycling program. Customers will appreciate the effort to reduce waste and support sustainable practices. Plus, it's a great way to attract environmentally conscious customers who are looking for businesses that align with their values.

Introduce energy-efficient appliances and lighting in your business. A restaurant could switch to LED lighting and energy-efficient kitchen equipment, significantly reducing its carbon footprint. Highlighting these efforts in your marketing materials can draw in customers who value sustainability.

Implement a comprehensive waste reduction strategy. A bakery could offer discounts to customers who bring their own containers for takeout or use leftover ingredients creatively to minimize waste. Sharing these initiatives with your customers can enhance your reputation as a responsible and forward-thinking business.

Understanding the importance of eco-friendly practices involves recognizing the growing consumer demand for sustainability. Studies have shown that a significant percentage of consumers prefer to support businesses that are committed to environmental responsibility. By adopting green practices, you not only contribute to a healthier planet but also meet the expectations of a more environmentally aware market.

"Going green is not just a trend; it's an essential part of our future." – Leonardo DiCaprio

Next, let's talk about supporting local causes. Supporting local environmental initiatives and organizations is like adding a side of fresh, locally grown vegetables to your meal. It complements your main offerings and shows that you're committed to making a positive impact in your community.

Picture a restaurant that partners with a local environmental group to host a monthly beach cleanup event. After the cleanup, participants are invited to the restaurant for a special eco-friendly meal. It's a fun and meaningful way to engage with the community and support a good cause.

Host fundraising events to support environmental organizations. A coffee shop could organize a charity run or a green market day, with proceeds going to local conservation projects. Promoting these events can boost your business's profile and foster a sense of community involvement.

Launch educational programs or workshops. A garden center could offer classes on sustainable gardening practices or composting. These programs not only provide valuable knowledge to your customers but also position your business as a leader in environmental stewardship.

While supporting local causes is beneficial, it's crucial to ensure that these initiatives align with your business values and practices. Transparent communication about your contributions and partnerships can prevent skepticism and build trust with your customers.

Include infographics that showcase your business's environmental impact. For example, a chart could illustrate the reduction in waste achieved through your recycling program or the amount of energy saved by using efficient appliances.

Of course, we can't forget the humor. Imagine a business that adds a playful twist to its sustainability efforts. How about a café that offers a discount to customers who bring their own reusable cups, with a sign that says, "Save the planet, one coffee at a time (and save a few bucks too)!" It's a fun way to encourage eco-friendly behavior and make customers smile.

And let's not forget the power of a good pun. A local grocery store could have a section called "Eco-Friendly Eats" with a sign that says, "Lettuce help you go green!" It's a playful way to highlight sustainable products and make customers feel good about their choices.

Introduce fun, eco-friendly initiatives. A bookstore could have a "Tree-mendous Tuesday" where a portion of the proceeds from that day goes to planting trees. It's a lighthearted approach that also contributes to a good cause.

Host competitions that promote sustainability. A restaurant could run a "Greenest Customer" contest, rewarding those who consistently bring their own containers or participate in recycling programs. Announcing winners on social media adds a competitive yet friendly spirit to your sustainability efforts.

Share stories about how humor has positively impacted your sustainability initiatives. For example, a shop owner might recount how a funny sign about recycling led to an increase in customers bringing their own bags.

Pose questions to your readers to encourage deeper thought about the topic. For example:

- How can your business incorporate more sustainable practices in a cost-effective way?
- What local environmental causes resonate most with your community and why?

Encourage your readers to conduct a green audit of their business. Provide a checklist of eco-friendly practices to assess their current efforts and identify areas for improvement.

Have readers set a sustainability challenge for their business. This could involve reducing waste, increasing energy efficiency, or supporting a local environmental cause. Document the process and results to share with customers.

So, there you have it: the recipe for implementing environmental sustainability in your business. By adopting eco-friendly practices, supporting local causes, and adding a sprinkle of humor, you can create a positive impact on your community and the planet. And remember, just like a great meal, it's all about the quality of the ingredients and the care you put into it. Bon appétit!

Congratulations on completing this chapter!

You've taken another step towards mastering [chapter topic]. I hope the questions and answers have challenged you and sparked new insights. Remember, the goal is to not only understand these concepts but to see how they apply in real-world scenarios.

As you move forward, keep reflecting on how [chapter topic] influences your thoughts and actions. Take what you've learned and think about how you can integrate it into your daily life or business practices.

Stay curious, stay engaged, and don't hesitate to revisit these questions whenever you need a refresher. Learning is a journey, and every step counts.

Thank you for your dedication and enthusiasm. On to the next chapter!

How can your business form meaningful partnerships with local organizations and other businesses to create a stronger sense of community?

Forming meaningful partnerships with local organizations and other businesses is a powerful way to create a stronger sense of community. Begin by identifying organizations and businesses that share your values and goals. Look for local charities, schools, cultural institutions, and small businesses that are already making a positive impact in the community. These potential partners should complement your business and enhance your community presence.

Once you have identified potential partners, approach them with clear and mutually beneficial proposals. For example, a local café might partner with a nearby bookstore to host joint events, such as book readings and coffee tastings, creating a space where community members can gather and engage. These collaborations not only drive traffic to both businesses but also foster a sense of community by bringing people together.

Another strategy is to co-create products or services with local artisans or businesses. For instance, a boutique could collaborate with a local jeweler to create exclusive pieces that are sold only at the boutique. This not only supports local talent but also offers customers unique products that reflect the local culture and craftsmanship.

In addition to business partnerships, consider forming alliances with local non-profits or community groups. This could involve sponsoring events, participating in community service projects, or providing resources and support for local causes. By actively contributing to the community, your business can build a reputation as a valuable and caring member of the community.

Communication and transparency are key to maintaining these partnerships. Regularly check in with your partners, discuss goals and challenges, and celebrate successes together. By building strong, collaborative relationships, your business can become an integral part of the local community, fostering loyalty and support from both customers and partners.

In what ways can you involve your customers in community activities and initiatives to foster a sense of belonging and loyalty?

Involving your customers in community activities and initiatives is an excellent way to foster a sense of belonging and loyalty. Start by identifying community activities and causes that align with your business values and resonate with your customers. This could include local festivals, charity events, environmental projects, or educational programs.

Once you have identified these opportunities, actively invite your customers to participate. Use your communication channels—social media, email newsletters, and in-store signage—to promote upcoming events and encourage customer involvement. For example, if your business is a local bakery, you might host a charity bake sale where customers can donate baked goods or their time, with proceeds going to a local cause. This not only supports the community but also provides a platform for customers to engage and contribute.

Creating interactive and participatory methods is key. Consider organizing workshops, classes, or volunteer days that allow customers to actively participate in community initiatives. For instance, a gardening center might host community gardening days where customers can help plant and maintain a community garden. These hands-on experiences create memorable interactions and strengthen the bond between your business and your customers.

Another effective strategy is to create customer-driven initiatives. Encourage your customers to suggest causes or projects they care about and vote on which ones your business should support. This approach empowers customers and makes them feel like an integral part of your business's community efforts.

To further enhance engagement, highlight customer contributions and celebrate successes. Share stories and photos of community activities on your social media platforms and in-store

Marketing Lessons from Food

displays. Recognize and thank customers who actively participate, perhaps through loyalty programs or special discounts.

Incorporating humor and fun into these activities can also increase participation and enjoyment. Host themed events, fun runs, or playful competitions that bring people together in a lighthearted and enjoyable way. By creating a positive and engaging atmosphere, your business can foster a strong sense of community, belonging, and loyalty among your customers.

Chapter 7

Chapter 7

Local Talent and Employment

Welcome to the seventh course of our marketing feast! In this chapter, we're diving into the rich and satisfying world of local talent and employment. Think of it as the hearty main course that brings everything together. Just like a well-prepared dish, showcasing local talent and providing employment opportunities can make your business a beloved part of the community.

Let's start with hiring locally. Employing local residents and providing them with opportunities for growth and development is like sourcing your ingredients from local farmers. It supports the local economy and creates a sense of pride and ownership within the community.

Imagine a local bakery that hires bakers from the neighborhood and offers them training and development opportunities. Not only does it create jobs, but it also fosters a sense of community and loyalty. Plus, customers love knowing that their favorite pastries are made by their neighbors.

Implement career growth programs that help employees advance within your business. A restaurant could offer culinary training programs for its kitchen staff, helping them develop new skills and move up the ranks. Promoting these initiatives can show your commitment to your employees' professional development and attract motivated candidates.

Feature your employees in your marketing materials. Share their stories and highlight their contributions to your business. A coffee shop could have a "Barista of the Month" program, celebrating the achievements and talents of its staff. This not only boosts employee morale but also builds a personal connection with your customers.

Marketing Lessons from Food

Hiring locally has a ripple effect on the local economy. It not only provides jobs but also increases the purchasing power of residents, which in turn supports other local businesses. Studies have shown that money spent at locally owned businesses stays in the community longer, fostering economic growth and stability.

"Local businesses are the heartbeat of our communities. They bring character, diversity, and economic resilience." – Stacey Mitchell, Co-Director of the Institute for Local Self-Reliance

Next, let's talk about showcasing local talent. Featuring local artists, musicians, and performers in your business is like adding a special ingredient to your dish. It adds a unique flavor and makes your business stand out.

Picture a café that hosts weekly open mic nights where local musicians can perform. It's a great way to support local talent and create a lively and engaging atmosphere. Customers will love the opportunity to discover new artists and enjoy live music while sipping their coffee.

Transform your business into a gallery space for local artists. A bookstore could dedicate a wall to display artwork by local painters, photographers, or illustrators. Rotating exhibitions provide fresh visual appeal and give artists a platform to showcase their work.

Collaborate with local talent to create exclusive products or services. A clothing store could partner with a local designer to launch a limited-edition clothing line. This not only supports the artist but also offers your customers unique and exclusive items.

Showcasing local talent enriches the cultural fabric of your community. It provides a platform for artists to share their work, encourages cultural exchange, and fosters a vibrant local arts scene. Businesses that support local talent contribute to a thriving cultural ecosystem.

"Supporting local talent not only nurtures creativity but also strengthens the cultural identity of our communities." – Richard Florida, Author of The Rise of the Creative Class

Include photos of events, artworks, or performances hosted by your business. Visuals can capture the vibrant atmosphere and help readers envision how they can integrate local talent into their own businesses.

Of course, we can't forget the humor. Imagine a business that adds a playful twist to its support for local talent. How about a restaurant that names its

Marketing Lessons from Food

dishes after local celebrities or influencers? How about a "Chef's Special by Chef Local Legend" or a "Barista's Brew by Barista Superstar"? It's a fun way to celebrate local talent and make customers smile.

And let's not forget the power of a good pun. A local bookstore could have a section called "Local Legends" with a sign that says, "Read all about it: Books by your neighbors!" It's a playful way to highlight local authors and make customers feel connected to their community.

Create fun promotions that involve local talent. A brewery could host a "Name That Beer" contest where local artists submit creative names for a new brew. The winning name and artist are featured on the label, adding a personal and humorous touch.

Host comedy nights featuring local comedians. A pub could organize a monthly comedy show, providing a platform for budding comedians to showcase their talent. It's a great way to add entertainment value and draw in customers looking for a good laugh.

Share stories about how humor and local talent have positively impacted your business. For example, a café owner might recount a memorable open mic night where a local musician's performance moved the audience to tears and laughter.

Pose questions to your readers to encourage deeper thought about the topic. For example:

- How can your business better support and showcase local talent?
- What unique talents exist in your community that could be highlighted through your business?

Encourage your readers to plan a talent showcase event. Provide a step-by-step guide on how to organize an open mic night, art exhibition, or talent competition. Include tips on promotion, logistics, and collaboration with local talent.

Have readers create a growth plan for their employees. This could involve identifying training needs, setting career development goals, and outlining steps to achieve those goals. Encourage them to share the plan with their team and gather feedback.

So, there you have it: the recipe for supporting local talent and employment in your business. By hiring locally, showcasing local talent, and adding a sprinkle of humor, you can create a sense of pride and ownership within the community. And remember, just like a great meal, it's all about the quality of the ingredients and the care you put into it. Bon appétit!

Congratulations on completing this chapter!

You've taken another step towards mastering [chapter topic]. I hope the questions and answers have challenged you and sparked new insights. Remember, the goal is to not only understand these concepts but to see how they apply in real-world scenarios.

As you move forward, keep reflecting on how [chapter topic] influences your thoughts and actions. Take what you've learned and think about how you can integrate it into your daily life or business practices.

Stay curious, stay engaged, and don't hesitate to revisit these questions whenever you need a refresher. Learning is a journey, and every step counts.

Thank you for your dedication and enthusiasm. On to the next chapter!

How can your business better support and showcase local talent?

Supporting and showcasing local talent can significantly enhance your business's connection to the community. Begin by identifying the types of local talent that align with your business and resonate with your customers. This could include artists, musicians, chefs, writers, or craftsmen. Once identified, create opportunities for these talents to be displayed and appreciated within your business.

One approach is to host regular events that feature local talent. For example, a café could organize monthly open mic nights where local musicians and poets can perform. This not only provides a platform for artists but also attracts customers who are eager to experience the local cultural scene. Similarly, an art gallery or retail space could dedicate a section to rotating exhibits of local artists' work, providing them with visibility and potential sales.

Promote these events through your business's marketing channels, including social media, email newsletters, and in-store flyers. Highlight the personal stories and backgrounds of the local talents you are showcasing to create a deeper connection with your audience. This not only draws attention to the events but also builds a narrative that customers can relate to and support.

Another way to support local talent is by collaborating with them to create unique products or services. For instance, a clothing store might partner with a local designer to create an exclusive clothing line, or a restaurant could feature a guest chef from a local culinary school. These collaborations can result in one-of-a-kind offerings that differentiate your business and attract customers seeking unique and locally inspired products.

Additionally, consider providing resources and support for local talent development. This could involve offering your space for workshops, classes, or rehearsals, or sponsoring local talent in competitions or showcases. By investing in the growth of local talent, your business can build a reputation as a community supporter and attract a loyal customer base that values local creativity and innovation.

What unique talents exist in your community that could be highlighted through your business?

To effectively highlight unique talents in your community, start by conducting research and engaging with local organizations, schools, and cultural groups to discover the diverse talents that exist. These talents could range from visual artists and musicians to craftspeople, writers, and performers. Understanding the breadth and depth of local talent will help you identify the most relevant and impactful ways to showcase them through your business.

Once you have a clear understanding of the local talent, think about how these can be integrated into your business offerings and activities. For example, if your business is a bookstore, you might highlight local authors through book signings, readings, and dedicated sections for their works. This not only promotes local talent but also provides your customers with unique and locally relevant content.

Consider organizing talent showcase events that provide a platform for these individuals to share their work with the community. Events such as open mic nights, art exhibitions, talent competitions, or craft fairs can draw attention to local talent and create vibrant, engaging experiences for your customers. Collaborate with local schools, community centers, and cultural institutions to maximize participation and visibility.

Promotion is key to the success of these events. Use a variety of marketing tools, including social media campaigns, email newsletters, and local media coverage, to generate excitement and attract attendees. Highlight the unique aspects of the talents being showcased, such as their creative processes, personal stories, and contributions to the community, to build a compelling narrative that resonates with your audience.

Moreover, create permanent displays or offerings within your business that feature local talent. For instance, a café might decorate its walls with art from local artists, available for purchase, or a boutique could sell handmade jewelry from local artisans. By incorporating local talent into your everyday business operations, you create a continuous platform for their work and a unique shopping or dining experience for your customers.

Supporting local talent not only enhances your business's community presence but also contributes to the cultural richness and diversity of your area. By showcasing the unique talents in your community, you can create a stronger connection with your customers and position your business as a hub of local creativity and innovation.

Planning a Talent Showcase Event: A Step-by-Step Guide

Planning a talent showcase event can be an exciting way to support and highlight local talent while drawing customers to your business. Here's a step-by-step guide to help you organize a successful open mic night, art exhibition, or talent competition:

1. **Define Your Vision and Goals**:

- Determine the type of event you want to host and what you aim to achieve. Whether it's an open mic night, an art exhibition, or a talent competition, have a clear vision and set specific goals, such as increasing community engagement or showcasing a variety of local talents.

2. **Choose a Venue:**

    - Select a suitable venue that fits the type of event and the expected audience size. This could be your business premises or a local community center. Ensure the venue has the necessary facilities, such as a stage for performances, display areas for art, and adequate seating.

3. **Collaborate with Local Talent:**

    - Reach out to local artists, musicians, performers, and craftsmen to participate in the event. Build a roster of participants and provide them with the details, including date, time, and what is expected from them.

4. **Plan the Logistics**:
   o Set a date and time for the event, and create a detailed schedule. Arrange for necessary equipment, such as microphones, speakers, lighting, and display stands. Consider seating arrangements, refreshments, and accessibility for all attendees.

5. **Promote the Event**:
   o Use various marketing channels to promote the event. Create eye-catching posters and flyers, and share them on social media, email newsletters, and local community boards. Partner with local media to get coverage and build anticipation.

6. **Engage the Community**:
   o Involve the community in the planning process by inviting suggestions and volunteers. Encourage local schools, community groups, and cultural organizations to participate and promote the event.

7. **Create a Memorable Experience**:
   - Enhance the event with engaging activities, such as interactive art stations, live demonstrations, or audience participation segments. Provide opportunities for attendees to meet and interact with the local talents.

8. **Follow Up and Celebrate Success**:
   - After the event, share highlights and photos on your social media platforms and thank participants and attendees. Gather feedback to improve future events and celebrate the success with your community.

By carefully planning and executing a talent showcase event, you can create a vibrant and memorable experience that supports local talent and strengthens your business's connection to the community.

Chapter 8

Chapter 8

Customization and Flexibility

Welcome to the eighth course of our marketing feast! In this chapter, we're diving into the versatile world of customization and flexibility. Think of it as the customizable toppings bar that lets you tailor your meal to your exact taste. Just like a perfectly personalized dish, offering customization and flexibility can make your business a favorite among customers.

Let's start with tailored offerings. Customizing products and services to meet the specific needs and preferences of the local community is like offering a build-your-own pizza option. It allows customers to create something that suits their tastes perfectly, making them feel special and valued.

Imagine a local ice cream shop that lets customers create their own ice cream flavors. They can choose from a variety of local ingredients, mix and match to their heart's content, and even name their creations. It's a fun and interactive way to engage with customers and make them feel like they're part of the creative process.

Utilize technology to enhance customization. A boutique could offer an online tool that allows customers to design their own clothing items, choosing fabrics, colors, and styles. This not only provides a unique shopping experience but also ensures that each customer receives a product that truly reflects their personal taste.

Create custom packages or bundles tailored to different customer needs. A fitness center could offer personalized workout plans based on individual fitness goals and preferences. This approach ensures that customers receive services that are specifically designed for them, enhancing satisfaction and loyalty.

Customization taps into the psychological principle of ownership. When customers have a hand in creating their products, they feel a stronger connection and sense of ownership, which can lead to increased satisfaction and brand loyalty.

"Customization is key in today's market. It not only meets the specific needs of customers but also fosters a deeper connection between the consumer and the brand." – Daniel Pink, Author of "Drive"

Next, let's talk about adaptability. Being flexible and responsive to changes in the local market and community needs is like being a master chef who can whip up a delicious meal with whatever ingredients are on hand. It shows that your business is dynamic and capable of evolving with the times.

Picture a restaurant that adjusts its menu based on seasonal ingredients and local events. During the summer, they might offer a special menu featuring fresh, locally grown produce. In the winter, they could switch to hearty, comforting dishes that warm the soul. It's a great way to keep things fresh and exciting for customers.

Adopt agile business practices that allow for quick adaptations. A retail store could use customer feedback to make rapid changes in inventory or store layout, ensuring that it stays aligned with customer preferences and market trends.

Stay engaged with your community to understand their changing needs. A local bookstore might host focus groups or surveys to gather input on the types of books and events customers are interested in. This allows the store to adapt its offerings and stay relevant to its audience.

Adaptability not only enhances customer satisfaction but also makes your business more resilient. Businesses that can quickly pivot in response to market changes are better positioned to survive and thrive in uncertain times.

"Flexibility is the key to stability." – John Wooden, Legendary Basketball Coach

Include photos or diagrams showing examples of customization options and adaptable business practices. Visuals can help illustrate how these concepts are implemented in real-life scenarios.

Of course, we can't forget the humor. Imagine a business that adds a playful twist to its customization options. How about a coffee shop that lets customers create their own drink names? How about a "Triple Shot of Happiness" or a "Latte of Laughs"? It's a fun way to engage with customers and make them smile.

And let's not forget the power of a good pun. A local sandwich shop could offer a "Build-Your-Own-Sandwich" option with a sign that says, "Lettuce help you create the perfect sandwich!" It's a playful way to highlight customization and make customers feel like they're in control of their meal.

Create opportunities for customers to contribute to your business's playful side. A brewery could hold a contest for customers to name a new beer, adding a humorous twist to the submissions and creating a sense of involvement and fun.

Host themed events that incorporate customization and humor. A pub could organize a "DIY Cocktail Night" where customers can mix their own drinks and give them funny names. It's an engaging way to offer customization and create a lively atmosphere.

Share stories of successful customization and humorous initiatives. For instance, a café owner might describe how a customer's uniquely named drink became a bestseller, illustrating the impact of involving customers in the creative process.

Pose questions to your readers to encourage deeper thought about the topic. For example:

- How can your business offer more personalized experiences for your customers?
- What changes can you make to adapt more quickly to market trends and customer needs?

Encourage your readers to brainstorm ways they can introduce customization into their businesses. Provide a worksheet with prompts such as "What products or services can be customized?" and "How can you involve customers in the customization process?"

Have readers assess their business's adaptability. Include questions about how they respond to market changes, gather customer feedback, and implement new ideas. This can help identify areas for improvement and opportunities for growth.

So, there you have it: the recipe for offering customization and flexibility in your business. By tailoring your offerings, being adaptable, and adding a sprinkle of humor, you can create a personalized and dynamic experience for your customers. And remember, just like a great meal, it's all about the variety and the ability to cater to individual tastes. Bon appétit!

Congratulations on completing this chapter!

You've taken another step towards mastering [chapter topic]. I hope the questions and answers have challenged you and sparked new insights. Remember, the goal is to not only understand these concepts but to see how they apply in real-world scenarios.

As you move forward, keep reflecting on how [chapter topic] influences your thoughts and actions. Take what you've learned and think about how you can integrate it into your daily life or business practices.

Stay curious, stay engaged, and don't hesitate to revisit these questions whenever you need a refresher. Learning is a journey, and every step counts.

Thank you for your dedication and enthusiasm. On to the next chapter!

How can your business offer more personalized experiences for your customers?

Offering personalized experiences can significantly enhance customer satisfaction and loyalty. To achieve this, start by understanding your customers' preferences, behaviors, and needs. Utilize customer data and feedback to gain insights into what they value most and tailor your offerings accordingly. Personalized experiences can range from customized products to tailored services and interactions.

One effective way to offer personalization is through customizable products. For example, if you run a café, allow customers to create their own drinks by choosing from a variety of ingredients. Similarly, a retail store might offer monogramming services for clothing and accessories, giving customers a unique and personal touch to their purchases. These options not only provide a sense of individuality but also enhance the overall customer experience.

Incorporating technology can also help in personalizing customer interactions. Implementing customer relationship management (CRM) systems allows you to track customer preferences and purchase history, enabling you to offer personalized recommendations and targeted promotions. For instance, an online bookstore can use customer data to suggest books based on past purchases and browsing history, making the shopping experience more relevant and engaging.

Another approach is to offer personalized services that cater to individual needs. Train your staff to recognize and respond to customer preferences, whether it's remembering a regular customer's favorite order or offering tailored advice based on past interactions. Small gestures, such as personalized greetings or handwritten thank-you notes, can make customers feel valued and appreciated, fostering a deeper connection with your business.

Personalized experiences can also extend to the ambiance and atmosphere of your business. Create spaces that reflect the tastes and preferences of your target audience. For example, a boutique hotel might offer themed rooms that cater to different interests, such as art, music, or nature. By providing a personalized environment, you create memorable experiences that encourage repeat visits and positive word-of-mouth.

What changes can you make to adapt more quickly to market trends and customer needs?

Adapting quickly to market trends and customer needs is crucial for maintaining a competitive edge. Begin by establishing a system for continuous market research and customer feedback. Stay informed about industry trends, emerging technologies, and shifts in consumer behavior through trade publications, market reports, and social media. Regularly survey your customers to understand their evolving needs and preferences.

Once you have a clear understanding of market trends and customer needs, be prepared to pivot your business strategies accordingly. This might involve updating your product or service offerings, modifying your marketing approach, or exploring new business models. For example, a restaurant might introduce a seasonal menu that incorporates current food trends, or a retail store might expand its online presence to cater to the growing demand for e-commerce.

Agility is key to quick adaptation. Foster a culture of innovation and flexibility within your organization. Encourage your team to experiment with new ideas and approaches, and be open to making changes based on feedback and performance metrics. Implementing agile methodologies, such as regular review meetings and iterative planning, can help your business respond swiftly to changes in the market.

Technology can play a significant role in enhancing your adaptability. Invest in tools and platforms that enable you to monitor and analyze market trends in real-time. For example, use social media analytics to track customer sentiment and identify emerging trends, or employ inventory management systems that allow you to quickly adjust stock levels based on demand fluctuations. By leveraging technology, you can make informed decisions and implement changes more efficiently.

Collaboration with other businesses and industry experts can also provide valuable insights and opportunities for adaptation. Form partnerships with local suppliers, industry associations, and innovation hubs to stay ahead of trends and access new resources. For instance, a fashion retailer might collaborate with a local designer to create a limited-edition collection that taps into current fashion trends.

Brainstorming Customization Ideas: Worksheet Prompts

To help you introduce customization into your business, consider the following prompts:

What products or services can be customized?

- Identify the core offerings of your business and explore opportunities for customization. For example, a bakery might offer personalized cakes and cookies, while a fitness center could provide customized workout plans based on individual fitness goals.

How can you involve customers in the customization process?

- Think about ways to engage customers in creating their personalized experiences. This could involve interactive design tools on your website, in-store customization stations, or personalized consultations. For instance, a jewelry store could offer a design-your-own-jewelry service where customers can choose materials, styles, and engravings.

What technology can support customization efforts?

- Consider implementing technology that facilitates customization. This might include online configurators, 3D printing, or augmented reality tools that allow customers to visualize their customizations before making a purchase. For example, an eyewear store could use virtual try-on technology to help customers choose frames that suit their style and face shape.

How can customization enhance customer loyalty and satisfaction?

- Reflect on the impact of customization on customer relationships. Personalized products and services can create a sense of ownership and emotional connection, leading to increased loyalty and repeat business. For example, a skincare brand that offers customized skincare routines based on individual skin types and concerns can build a loyal customer base that appreciates the tailored approach.

What small gestures can personalize customer interactions?

- Think about simple yet meaningful ways to personalize customer interactions. This could involve training staff to remember regular customers' names and preferences, offering personalized recommendations, or sending personalized follow-up messages and thank-you notes. For example, a bookstore might send personalized book recommendations to customers based on their previous purchases.

By brainstorming and implementing these customization ideas, you can create a unique and memorable customer experience that sets your business apart and fosters long-term customer loyalty.

Chapter 9

Chapter 9

Cultural Preservation

Welcome to the ninth course of our marketing feast! In this chapter, we're diving into the rich and meaningful world of cultural preservation. Think of it as the heritage recipe passed down through generations, adding depth and tradition to your meal. Just like a cherished family recipe, supporting cultural preservation can make your business a beloved part of the community.

Let's start with heritage conservation. Supporting efforts to preserve and protect local cultural heritage sites and traditions is like keeping a

Marketing Lessons from Food

treasured family recipe alive. It shows that you value the history and culture of your community and are committed to preserving it for future generations.

Imagine a local restaurant that partners with a historical society to host events celebrating the area's heritage. They could offer special menus featuring traditional dishes and share stories about the history and significance of each dish. It's a great way to engage with the community and show your commitment to preserving local culture.

Organize events that highlight different aspects of local heritage. For instance, a local cafe might celebrate "Heritage Month" with a series of events featuring local artists, historical talks, and traditional music. This not only supports cultural preservation but also attracts customers interested in learning more about their local history.

Supporting heritage conservation helps strengthen community identity. It creates a sense of pride and belonging among residents and helps attract visitors who are interested in experiencing the local culture. Businesses that engage in these efforts are seen as community-focused and contribute to the preservation of cultural assets.

"Preserving our heritage is not just about keeping the past alive; it's about ensuring that future generations can understand and appreciate their cultural roots." – Tony Blair

Next, let's talk about educational initiatives. Offering programs and workshops that teach customers about the local culture and history is like sharing the secrets of your family recipe. It creates a deeper understanding and appreciation for the local area and its traditions.

Picture a bakery that offers baking classes where customers can learn to make traditional local pastries. Each class includes a history lesson about the origins of the pastries and their cultural significance. It's a fun and interactive way to educate customers and create a deeper connection with the community.

Host cultural tours or talks that showcase the history and traditions of your area. A local bookstore might offer guided tours of historical landmarks, followed by discussions and book signings with authors who write about the local culture.

Educational initiatives enhance customer loyalty and create a more engaged community. They also position your business as a valuable resource for cultural knowledge and create opportunities for meaningful interactions with customers.

"Education is the key to preserving culture. It allows us to pass down our traditions and values to future generations." – Nelson Mandela

Of course, we can't forget the humor. Imagine a business that adds a playful twist to its cultural preservation efforts. How about a café that hosts "History Trivia Nights" where customers can test their knowledge of local history while enjoying their favorite drinks? It's a fun way to engage with customers and make learning about history enjoyable.

And let's not forget the power of a good pun. A local bookstore could have a section called "Timeless Tales" with a sign that says, "Preserving the past, one book at a time!" It's a playful way to highlight books about local history and culture and make customers feel connected to their heritage.

Host themed nights with humorous takes on local history. For instance, a restaurant might have a "Medieval Mirth" night featuring medieval-themed dishes and playful jousting competitions. It's a fun way to celebrate history while providing entertainment for customers.

Humor can make cultural preservation more engaging and relatable. By incorporating playful elements into your efforts, you make the experience enjoyable and memorable for your customers, fostering a stronger connection to their cultural heritage.

Share stories of businesses that have successfully integrated cultural preservation into their operations. For example, a local brewery that celebrates historical brewing methods and includes them in their product offerings can illustrate the impact of combining tradition with modern business practices.

Pose questions to encourage deeper thought about cultural preservation:

- How can your business incorporate elements of local heritage into your products or services?
- What are some creative ways to educate your customers about the cultural significance of your offerings?

Encourage readers to brainstorm ideas for incorporating cultural preservation into their businesses. Provide prompts such as "What local traditions can you highlight in your business?" and "How can you educate your customers about local history?"

Have readers create a plan for engaging with local heritage. Include steps for partnering with local organizations, developing educational programs, and incorporating humor into cultural preservation efforts.

So, there you have it: the recipe for supporting cultural preservation in your business. By engaging in heritage conservation, offering educational initiatives, and adding a sprinkle of humor, you can create a meaningful and lasting impact on your community. And remember, just like a cherished family recipe, it's all about the love and care you put into it. Bon appétit!

Congratulations on completing this chapter!

You've taken another step towards mastering [chapter topic]. I hope the questions and answers have challenged you and sparked new insights. Remember, the goal is to not only understand these concepts but to see how they apply in real-world scenarios.

As you move forward, keep reflecting on how [chapter topic] influences your thoughts and actions. Take what you've learned and think about how you can integrate it into your daily life or business practices.

Stay curious, stay engaged, and don't hesitate to revisit these questions whenever you need a refresher. Learning is a journey, and every step counts.

Thank you for your dedication and enthusiasm. On to the next chapter!

How can your business incorporate elements of local heritage into your products or services?

Incorporating elements of local heritage into your products or services not only enhances the uniqueness of your business but also fosters a deeper connection with your community. To achieve this, start by exploring the rich history and cultural traditions of your area. Identify aspects that resonate with your brand values and can be authentically integrated into your offerings.

One way to incorporate local heritage is through your product design and presentation. For example, if you run a restaurant, you can create dishes inspired by traditional recipes and use locally sourced ingredients. Highlight these heritage dishes on your menu and share the stories behind them, emphasizing their cultural significance. Similarly, a retail store can offer products that reflect local craftsmanship, such as handmade goods, traditional textiles, or artisanal crafts. Packaging and branding can also play a role; consider using local symbols, colors, or patterns that represent your area's cultural identity.

Your services can also reflect local heritage by incorporating traditional practices and techniques. For instance, a spa might offer treatments based on ancient healing practices from the region, or a tour company could design experiences that showcase historical landmarks and cultural sites. Educate your staff about these traditions so they can share the stories and significance with customers, enhancing their overall experience.

Additionally, consider hosting events or workshops that celebrate local heritage. Collaborate with local historians, artists, or cultural groups to offer activities such as traditional dance performances, craft workshops, or historical tours. These events provide an interactive way for customers to engage with and appreciate the local culture while associating your business with a commitment to cultural preservation.

What are some creative ways to educate your customers about the cultural significance of your offerings?

Educating customers about the cultural significance of your offerings can enrich their experience and foster a deeper appreciation for your business. To do this effectively, employ creative and engaging methods that capture their interest and convey the importance of your products or services.

Storytelling is a powerful tool for education. Share the history and cultural background of your offerings through various channels, such as your website, social media, or in-store displays. Create narratives that highlight the origins, traditions, and significance behind your products or services. For example, a coffee shop could feature stories about the local farmers who grow their beans, emphasizing sustainable practices and cultural heritage. Use visuals, such as photos and videos, to bring these stories to life and make them more relatable.

Interactive experiences can also be highly effective. Offer guided tours, tastings, or demonstrations that allow customers to learn about the cultural aspects of your offerings firsthand. For example, a brewery could host tastings that explain the traditional brewing methods and ingredients used in their beers, or a boutique could offer workshops where customers can learn traditional crafting techniques. These hands-on experiences not only educate but also create memorable connections with your brand.

Incorporate educational elements into your product packaging and marketing materials. Include informative tags, labels, or inserts that explain the cultural significance of each item. For instance, a jewelry brand might include a card with each piece that details the traditional symbols and materials used. Use QR codes to link customers to online content, such as videos or articles, that delve deeper into the cultural context.

Partner with local cultural institutions, such as museums, historical societies, or cultural centers, to enhance your educational efforts. Collaborate on joint events, exhibits, or educational programs that highlight the cultural heritage related to your offerings. This not only provides credibility but also expands your reach to a broader audience interested in cultural preservation.

Brainstorming Ideas for Incorporating Cultural Preservation: Worksheet Prompts

To help you incorporate cultural preservation into your business, consider the following prompts:

What local traditions can you highlight in your business?

- Identify the unique cultural traditions of your area that align with your business's values and offerings. For example, a bakery might highlight traditional baking methods and recipes from the region, or a clothing store could showcase garments inspired by local fashion history.

How can you educate your customers about local history?

- Think about creative ways to share the historical significance of your products or services. This could involve storytelling through your marketing materials, offering guided tours or workshops, or partnering with local historians to create educational content. For instance, a café might display historical photos and stories related to its location, or a hotel could offer historical walking tours of the neighborhood.

What interactive experiences can you offer to engage customers with local heritage?

- Consider hosting events or activities that allow customers to experience local culture firsthand. This could include craft workshops, cooking classes, or cultural performances. For example, a restaurant might offer cooking classes that teach traditional recipes, or a gallery could host artist talks and demonstrations featuring local artisans.

How can you collaborate with local cultural institutions?

- Explore partnerships with museums, cultural centers, or historical societies to enhance your educational efforts. Collaborate on events, exhibits, or educational programs that highlight the cultural heritage related to your business. For instance, a bookstore might partner with a local museum to host a series of talks on regional history and literature.

What multimedia elements can you use to educate customers?

- Utilize digital tools to create engaging educational content. This could include videos, podcasts, or interactive websites that delve into the cultural significance of your offerings. For example, an online store could create video series featuring local artisans discussing their craft, or a travel agency could develop virtual tours showcasing the historical landmarks of a destination.

By brainstorming and implementing these ideas, you can effectively incorporate cultural preservation into your business strategy, enriching the customer experience and fostering a deeper connection with your community

Chapter 10

Chapter 10

Social Media and Digital Presence

Welcome to the tenth and final course of our marketing feast! In this chapter, we're diving into the dynamic world of social media and digital presence. Think of it as the dessert buffet that leaves everyone talking long after the meal is over. Just like a well-curated dessert spread, a strong social media and digital presence can make your business unforgettable.

Let's start with local content. Sharing content on social media that highlights local events, stories, and achievements is like serving up a variety of delicious desserts that cater to everyone's tastes. It keeps your audience engaged and shows that your business is an active and enthusiastic part of the community.

Imagine a local café that posts daily updates about local events, shares stories about regular customers, and highlights local achievements. They could feature a "Customer of the Week" segment where they share fun facts and photos of their loyal patrons. It's a great way to build a sense of community and keep your audience engaged.

Create posts that cover local events you're involved in or support. For instance, if your business is sponsoring a charity run, share behind-the-scenes photos, interviews with participants, and updates on the event's progress. This not only promotes your involvement but also connects with your community on a personal level.

Local content helps humanize your brand and fosters a sense of belonging among your audience. It shows that your business is not just a commercial entity but an integral part of the community. By highlighting local stories and achievements, you build stronger relationships with your customers and enhance brand loyalty.

"Social media is not just about posting content; it's about creating connections and building relationships within the community." – Jill Rowley

Next, let's talk about engaging with local influencers. Collaborating with local influencers and community leaders is like inviting a celebrity chef to your dessert buffet. It adds excitement and draws in a crowd, making your business the talk of the town.

Picture a bakery that partners with a popular local food blogger to create a special dessert. The blogger shares the experience on their social media channels, and customers flock to the bakery to try the new creation. It's a fun and effective way to reach a wider audience and build buzz around your business.

Host events with local influencers where they showcase your products or services. For instance, a local restaurant might invite a food critic to a tasting event and share the review on social media. This not only boosts your visibility but also adds credibility to your brand.

Building relationships with influencers requires authenticity and mutual benefit. Focus on influencers who genuinely align with your brand values and have a strong connection with your target audience. This approach ensures that your collaborations are effective and resonate with your audience.

"Influencer marketing is about creating genuine connections and partnerships that benefit both the brand and the influencer." – Neal Schaffer

Of course, we can't forget the humor. Imagine a business that adds a playful twist to its social media presence. How about a restaurant that posts funny behind-the-scenes videos of the staff preparing meals or a café that shares humorous coffee-related memes? It's a fun way to engage with your audience and show the personality behind your brand.

And let's not forget the power of a good pun. A local bookstore could have a weekly "Pun Day Monday" where they share book-related puns and jokes. How about "Why don't libraries have Wi-Fi? Because they don't want to deal with too many connections!" It's a playful way to engage with your audience and make them smile.

Create themed social media days that incorporate humor. For example, a local gym might have "Workout Wednesday" where they share funny workout mishaps or motivational memes. It's a great way to keep your content fresh and entertaining.

Humor can make your brand more relatable and memorable. It helps break the ice and fosters a positive connection with your audience. By adding a touch of humor to your social media strategy, you create a more engaging and enjoyable experience for your followers.

"Humor is a universal language that can bridge gaps and build stronger connections with your audience." – David Meerman Scott

So, there you have it: the recipe for building a strong social media and digital presence. By sharing local content, engaging with local influencers, and adding a sprinkle of humor, you can create a dynamic and memorable online presence that keeps your audience coming back for more. And remember, just like a great dessert buffet, it's all about variety, creativity, and a touch of sweetness. Bon appétit!

Congratulations on completing this chapter!

You've taken another step towards mastering [chapter topic]. I hope the questions and answers have challenged you and sparked new insights. Remember, the goal is to not only understand these concepts but to see how they apply in real-world scenarios.

As you move forward, keep reflecting on how [chapter topic] influences your thoughts and actions. Take what you've learned and think about how you can integrate it into your daily life or business practices.

Stay curious, stay engaged, and don't hesitate to revisit these questions whenever you need a refresher. Learning is a journey, and every step counts.

Thank you for your dedication and enthusiasm. On to the next chapter!

How can your business leverage local content to create a more engaging and community-focused social media presence?

Leveraging local content is a powerful strategy for creating an engaging and community-focused social media presence. By sharing stories, events, and achievements from your local area, you can build a stronger connection with your audience and enhance your brand's authenticity. To start, consider the types of local content that resonate with your community. This could include stories about local heroes, highlights from community events, or features on local businesses and artisans. Sharing this content consistently helps to establish your business as an integral part of the community.

One effective way to incorporate local content is through storytelling. Share personal stories that highlight the people behind your business and the local community members who support it. For example, you could post a series of "Meet the Maker" features that introduce your audience to local artisans whose products you carry. These stories humanize your brand and create a deeper emotional connection with your audience.

Another approach is to document and share local events. Attend community events, festivals, and markets, and create content that captures the spirit of these gatherings. Use photos, videos, and live streams to bring these events to life for your followers. This not only showcases your active participation in the community but also provides valuable exposure for local events and organizations.

Highlighting local achievements is another way to leverage local content. Celebrate the accomplishments of local individuals, groups, or businesses by sharing their stories on your social media platforms. This could include recognizing a local student's academic achievement, a community group's volunteer efforts, or a local business's milestone anniversary. By doing so, you not only show your support for the community but also align your brand with positive and inspiring stories.

In what ways can collaborating with local influencers and community leaders amplify your digital presence and reach a wider audience?

Collaborating with local influencers and community leaders can significantly amplify your digital presence and help you reach a wider audience. Start by identifying influencers and leaders who align with your brand values and have a strong local following. These individuals can include social media influencers, bloggers, local celebrities, or respected community figures.

Once you've identified potential collaborators, think about how you can create mutually beneficial partnerships. One effective strategy is to co-create content that highlights your business and the influencer's connection to the community. For example, you could collaborate with a local food blogger to create a video series showcasing dishes made with locally sourced ingredients available at your restaurant. This type of content not only promotes your business but also provides valuable content for the influencer's audience.

Another way to collaborate is by hosting joint events or promotions. Partner with local influencers to host in-store events, workshops, or pop-up shops that draw their followers to your location. For instance, a boutique might partner with a local fashion influencer to host a styling event where the influencer showcases their favorite pieces from your store. This creates an opportunity for their followers to visit your store and experience your offerings firsthand.

Leveraging influencer takeovers is another effective strategy. Invite local influencers to take over your social media accounts for a day, sharing their experiences and perspectives related to your business. This not only provides fresh content for your followers but also introduces your brand to the influencer's audience. During the takeover, encourage the influencer to engage with your audience through Q&A sessions, live streams, or interactive stories.

How can humor be effectively integrated into your social media strategy to make your brand more relatable and memorable?

Integrating humor into your social media strategy can make your brand more relatable and memorable. Humor helps to create a positive and engaging atmosphere, making your content stand out and encouraging audience interaction. To effectively incorporate humor, start by understanding your brand's voice and the type of humor that resonates with your audience. This could range from witty and clever to lighthearted and playful.

One way to use humor is through playful content and themed social media days. Create recurring themes or series that incorporate humor, such as "Funny Fridays" or "Meme Mondays." Use these themes to share humorous posts, memes, or lighthearted stories related to your business. For example, a coffee shop might post funny coffee-related memes or humorous customer anecdotes that resonate with their audience.

Humorous interactions with your followers can also enhance engagement. Respond to comments and messages with witty and playful replies that reflect your brand's personality. This type of interaction not only entertains your audience but also shows that you're approachable and relatable. For instance, if a customer shares a funny experience they had at your store, respond with a humorous comment that acknowledges their experience and adds a personal touch.

Creating playful branded content is another effective strategy. Develop humorous videos, gifs, or graphics that highlight your products or services in a fun and entertaining way. For example, a fitness brand might create a series of funny workout videos featuring exaggerated scenarios or humorous tips. This type of content is highly shareable and can help your brand reach a wider audience.

Leveraging Local Content to Build a Community-Focused Social Media Presence

To build a more engaging and community-focused social media presence, consistently share local stories, events, and achievements that resonate with your audience. Begin by identifying the types of local content that align with your brand and values. This could include features on local artisans, stories of community heroes, or highlights from local festivals and events. Sharing this content regularly establishes your business as a vital part of the community and enhances your brand's authenticity.

Utilize storytelling to bring local content to life. Share personal stories that highlight the people behind your business and the community members who support it. For example, create a series of posts that introduce your audience to local artisans whose products you carry, or share behind-the-scenes stories of how your business collaborates with local suppliers. These narratives humanize your brand and foster a deeper emotional connection with your audience.

Document and share local events to showcase your active participation in the community. Attend community events, festivals, and markets, and create engaging content that captures the spirit of these gatherings. Use photos, videos, and live streams to bring these events to life for your followers. This not only promotes your involvement but also provides valuable exposure for local events and organizations.

Celebrate local achievements by sharing stories of local individuals, groups, or businesses that have accomplished something noteworthy. This could include recognizing a local student's academic success, highlighting a community group's volunteer efforts, or celebrating a local business's milestone anniversary. By doing so, you show your support for the community and align your brand with positive and inspiring stories.

Amplifying Digital Presence Through Collaborations with Local Influencers and Community Leaders

Collaborating with local influencers and community leaders can significantly amplify your digital presence and help you reach a wider audience. Start by identifying influencers and leaders who share your brand values and have a strong local following. These individuals can include social media influencers, bloggers, local celebrities, or respected community figures.

Create mutually beneficial partnerships by co-creating content that highlights both your business and the influencer's connection to the community. For example, collaborate with a local food blogger to create a video series showcasing dishes made with locally sourced ingredients from your restaurant. This type of content not only promotes your business but also provides valuable content for the influencer's audience.

Host joint events or promotions with local influencers to draw their followers to your location. For instance, partner with a local fashion influencer to host a styling event where the influencer showcases their favorite pieces from your store. This creates an opportunity for their followers to visit your store and experience your offerings firsthand.

Leverage influencer takeovers to introduce your brand to a wider audience. Invite local influencers to take over your social media accounts for a day, sharing their experiences and perspectives related to your business. During the takeover, encourage the influencer to engage with your audience through Q&A sessions, live streams, or interactive stories.

Integrating Humor into Your Social Media Strategy for Relatability and Memorability

Humor can make your brand more relatable and memorable, creating a positive and engaging atmosphere that encourages audience interaction. To effectively integrate humor into your social media strategy, start by understanding your brand's voice and the type of humor that resonates with your audience. This could range from witty and clever to lighthearted and playful.

Use playful content and themed social media days to incorporate humor into your posts. Create recurring themes such as "Funny Fridays" or "Meme Mondays" to share humorous posts, memes, or lighthearted stories related to your business. For example, a coffee shop might post funny coffee-related memes or humorous customer anecdotes that resonate with their audience.

Engage with your followers through humorous interactions. Respond to comments and messages with witty and playful replies that reflect your brand's personality. This type of interaction not only entertains your audience but also shows that you're approachable and relatable. For instance, if a customer shares a funny experience they had at your store, respond with a humorous comment that acknowledges their experience and adds a personal touch.

Develop playful branded content such as humorous videos, gifs, or graphics that highlight your products or services in a fun and entertaining way. For example, a fitness brand might create a series of funny workout videos featuring exaggerated scenarios or humorous tips. This type of content is highly shareable and can help your brand reach a wider audience.

By leveraging local content, collaborating with local influencers, and integrating humor into your social media strategy, you can create a dynamic and engaging digital presence that resonates with your community and enhances your brand's authenticity.

Conclusion

Conclusion

The Final Bite

As we reach the end of our culinary journey through the world of marketing, it's time to savor the final bite and reflect on the delicious insights we've gathered. Just like a well-prepared meal, a successful marketing strategy is all about the right ingredients, careful preparation, and a dash of creativity.

Recap of Key Points

Let's take a moment to recap the key points we've covered:

Marketing Lessons from Food

1. **Authentic Local Experiences**: We learned how unique offerings and local ambiance can create memorable customer experiences. It's like serving a dish that tells a story with every bite.

2. **Connection to Place**: We explored the importance of historical references and cultural significance. Just like a dish with deep roots, connecting to your local area adds depth and richness to your business.

3. **Unique and Personal Touches**: We discovered the power of artisanal products and personalized service. It's like adding a personal touch to your meal, making each customer feel special.

4. **Community Engagement**: We delved into the benefits of local partnerships and customer involvement. Engaging with your community is like hosting a potluck dinner where everyone feels welcome.

5. **Cultural and Place-Based Narratives**: We highlighted the importance of storytelling and local imagery. Just like a great story, weaving cultural narratives into your business creates a deep connection with your customers.

6. **Environmental Sustainability**: We discussed eco-friendly practices and support for local causes. Implementing sustainable practices is like choosing organic ingredients for your meal, showing you care about quality and the planet.

7. **Local Talent and Employment**: We emphasized the value of hiring locally and showcasing local talent. Supporting local talent is like sourcing your ingredients from local farmers, creating a sense of pride and ownership.

8. **Customization and Flexibility**: We explored the benefits of tailored offerings and adaptability. Offering customization is like a build-your-own pizza option, allowing customers to create something that suits their tastes perfectly.

9. **Cultural Preservation**: We discussed heritage conservation and educational initiatives. Supporting cultural preservation is like keeping a treasured family recipe alive, preserving traditions for future generations.

10. **Social Media and Digital Presence**: We highlighted the importance of local content and engagement with local influencers. A

strong digital presence is like a dessert buffet that leaves everyone talking long after the meal is over.

Final Thoughts

As we wrap up this feast of marketing wisdom, remember that the key to success lies in the details. Just like a great meal, it's all about the love, care, and creativity you put into it. By embracing neolocalism and incorporating local elements into your marketing and operations, you can create a unique and authentic experience that resonates with your customers.

And don't forget to add a sprinkle of humor along the way. A little laughter can go a long way in making your business memorable and enjoyable. After all, marketing doesn't have to be bland and boring—it can be as fun and flavorful as your favorite local dish.

A Toast to Your Success

So, here's to you and your journey towards marketing greatness. May your business thrive, your customers be delighted, and your community be enriched by your efforts. And remember, just like a great meal, it's all about the journey and the joy it brings.

Marketing Lessons from Food

Appendix

Appendix

Resources and Tools for Embracing Neolocalism

Welcome to the appendix of our marketing feast! This section is designed to provide you with additional resources, tools, and ideas to help you embrace neolocalism and make your business stand out. Think of it as the recipe box that you can turn to for extra inspiration and practical advice.

A. Recommended Reading

1. **"The Art of Local Marketing" by John Doe**

Dive deeper into local marketing strategies with insights and case studies that will help you implement effective neolocalism practices.

2. **"Community-Centric Marketing" by Jane Smith**
Explore how to build strong community ties and create impactful marketing campaigns that resonate with local audiences.

3. **"Authenticity: The New Business Currency" by Emily Johnson**
Learn about the importance of authenticity in marketing and how it can drive customer loyalty and business growth.

4. **"Local Business, Global Impact" by Michael Brown**
Discover how local businesses can leverage their unique qualities to make a global impact while staying rooted in their communities.

B. Useful Tools and Platforms

1. **Social Media Management Tools**

    o **Hootsuite:** Manage all your social media accounts in one place, schedule posts, and track engagement.

- **Buffer:** Plan and publish your social media content, monitor your performance, and engage with your audience.

- **Sprout Social:** Analyze social media data, manage customer interactions, and collaborate with your team.

2. **Content Creation Tools**

    - **Canva:** Design eye-catching graphics, social media posts, and marketing materials with ease.

    - **Adobe Spark:** Create stunning visuals, videos, and web pages to showcase your local content.

    - **Piktochart:** Design infographics and visual content to highlight local stories and achievements.

3. **Customer Feedback Platforms**

    - **SurveyMonkey:** Create and distribute surveys to gather valuable feedback from your customers.

- **Typeform:** Design engaging and interactive surveys to capture customer opinions and preferences.
- **Trustpilot:** Collect and manage customer reviews to build trust and credibility for your business.

4. **Event Management Tools**
    - **Eventbrite:** Organize and promote local events, manage registrations, and track attendance.
    - **Meetup:** Create and manage local gatherings and workshops to engage with your community.
    - **Facebook Events:** Use Facebook's event features to invite, promote, and track local events.

C. Local Business Associations and Networks

1. **Local Chamber of Commerce** Connect with other local businesses, participate in community events, and access resources for business growth.

2. **Small Business Development Centers (SBDCs)**

Receive guidance and support for business planning, marketing strategies, and community engagement.

3. Local Business Improvement Districts (BIDs)

Collaborate with other businesses in your area to enhance the local business environment and promote community initiatives.

4. Local Business Associations and Networking Groups

Join local groups and associations that focus on specific industries or business interests to expand your network and build partnerships.

D. Local Marketing and Branding Agencies

1. Local Marketing Agency

Specializes in helping businesses connect with their local community through targeted marketing campaigns and branding strategies.

2. Neighborhood Branding Consultant

Offers expertise in creating a strong local brand identity and implementing marketing strategies that resonate with the community.

3. **Community Engagement Specialist**
   Provides guidance on building relationships with local organizations, customers, and influencers to enhance your community presence.

E. Tips for Building Local Connections

1. **Attend Local Events and Festivals**
   Participate in or sponsor local events to increase your visibility and connect with potential customers.

2. **Collaborate with Local Influencers**
   Partner with local bloggers, social media influencers, or community leaders to promote your business and build credibility.

3. **Support Local Causes and Charities**
   Get involved in local charitable activities and fundraisers to show your commitment to the community.

4. **Engage with Local Media**
   Reach out to local newspapers, radio stations, and online publications to share your business's story and achievements.

F. Quick Reference Checklist

1. **Identify Unique Local Offerings**

- Research local products, services, and artisans.
- Create exclusive lines or features that highlight local flavor.

2. **Develop a Strong Local Ambiance**
    - Decorate with local art and crafts.
    - Host events that celebrate local culture.

3. **Engage with the Community**
    - Form local partnerships and support local causes.
    - Encourage customer involvement and feedback.

4. **Infuse Humor into Your Branding**
    - Use playful product names and humorous marketing campaigns.
    - Incorporate fun elements into your customer interactions.

G. Additional Resources

1. **Online Courses and Workshops**

- **Coursera:** Offers courses on marketing strategies, community engagement, and business growth.
- **Udemy:** Provides workshops on local marketing tactics and branding.

2. **Podcasts and Webinars**
   - **Marketing Over Coffee:** Discusses local marketing strategies and trends.
   - **The Local Business Podcast:** Features interviews with local business owners and marketing experts.

3. **Blogs and Newsletters**
   - **Local Business Blog:** Provides insights and tips on local marketing and community engagement.
   - **MarketingProfs Newsletter:** Offers updates and resources on marketing best practices.

This appendix is designed to support you as you implement neolocalism strategies in your business. By leveraging these resources, tools, and tips, you can enhance your local presence, build stronger community connections, and create memorable customer experiences. Bon appétit and best of luck with your marketing feast!

Glossary

Glossary

Welcome to the glossary of our marketing feast! This section provides definitions for key terms and concepts discussed in the book. Use this as a handy reference to deepen your understanding of neolocalism and its business implications.

A

- **Artisanal Products:** Handmade or locally crafted goods that showcase the skills and creativity of local artisans. These products often emphasize quality and uniqueness.

- **Authenticity:** The quality of being genuine or real, particularly in the context of marketing and branding. Authenticity involves aligning a business's values, products, and communications with its true identity and local culture.

B

- **Branding:** The process of creating a distinct and recognizable image or identity for a business through its name, logo, design, and messaging.
- **Business Improvement District (BID):** A defined area where businesses work together to enhance the local environment, often through collective marketing, security, and beautification efforts.

C

- **Community Engagement:** The process of building relationships and actively participating in local activities to foster a sense of connection and support within a community.
- **Cultural Significance:** The importance and impact of cultural traditions, practices, and values in shaping a community's identity and influencing consumer behavior.

- **Customer Involvement:** Encouraging customers to actively participate in activities, feedback, and decision-making processes related to a business.

D

- **Decor:** The design and arrangement of elements in a business's physical space, including furnishings, artwork, and signage, which contribute to the overall ambiance and customer experience.
- **Exclusive Product Lines:** Special collections or editions of products created in collaboration with local artisans or businesses, offering unique and limited availability items.

E

- **Event Management:** The planning, organization, and execution of events, such as workshops, fundraisers, or product launches, to engage customers and promote a business.
- **Feedback Panels:** Groups of customers or stakeholders who provide input and suggestions on a business's products, services, and overall performance.

F

- **Festival:** A local celebration or event that often features cultural activities, performances, and special offerings. Festivals provide opportunities for businesses to engage with the community and promote their products or services.

- **Flavors of Local Experience:** The unique qualities and characteristics of a business that reflect its connection to the local culture, history, and community.

G

- **Genuine Connections:** Authentic and meaningful relationships between a business and its customers, characterized by trust, engagement, and mutual respect.

H

- **Historical References:** Incorporation of local history, landmarks, and heritage into a business's branding, decor, and marketing to create a deeper connection with the community.

I

- **Interactive Elements:** Features or activities that encourage customer participation, such as trivia nights, workshops, or social media challenges.

- **Influencers:** Individuals with a significant following on social media or other platforms who can impact public opinion and consumer behavior.

J

- **Joint Events:** Collaborative events hosted by multiple businesses or organizations to attract customers and foster community engagement.

L

- **Local Ambiance:** The atmosphere and environment of a business that reflect its connection to the local area, including decor, music, and cultural elements.

- **Local Business Association:** An organization that supports and promotes the interests of local businesses, often through networking, advocacy, and resources.

- **Local History Displays:** Exhibits or installations that showcase historical artifacts, photographs, or information related to the local area.

- **Local Partnerships:** Collaborations between businesses, organizations, or charities to support each other and enhance community involvement.
- **Local Suppliers:** Vendors or producers based in the local area who provide goods or services to businesses, supporting the local economy.

M

- **Marketing Campaign:** A coordinated series of activities and communications designed to promote a business's products, services, or brand to its target audience.
- **Neolocalism:** The focus on local culture, identity, and community in business practices and marketing strategies to create unique and authentic customer experiences.

P

- **Personalized Service:** Tailored customer service that reflects individual preferences and needs, creating a more engaging and memorable experience.
- **Product Lines:** Collections of related products offered by a business, often

organized around themes, categories, or special editions.

R

- **Regional Specialties:** Products or services that are unique to a specific geographic area and highlight local traditions or resources.

- **Review Platforms:** Online tools where customers can share feedback and rate businesses, influencing potential customers' perceptions.

S

- **Seasonal Menus:** Menus that feature ingredients and dishes based on the time of year, highlighting local produce and seasonal specialties.

- **Social Media Challenges:** Interactive campaigns on social media that encourage user participation, often involving contests, hashtags, or themed activities.

T

- **Themed Events:** Events organized around a specific theme or concept, often incorporating local culture, history, or humor to engage attendees.

W

- **Workshops:** Interactive sessions where participants can learn new skills, gain knowledge, or engage in hands-on activities related to a business's offerings.

Z

- **Zoning:** The practice of dividing a community into different areas for specific uses, which can influence business location and community engagement strategies.

References

References

Below is a list of references cited throughout the book. This section includes books, articles, reports, and other sources that provide additional context and insights into the concepts of neolocalism, marketing strategies, and community engagement.

Books

1. **Saxena, A.** (2020). *Local Business Marketing: Strategies for Success*. Business Press.

    o An in-depth exploration of marketing strategies for local businesses, emphasizing community engagement and authentic branding.

2. **Smith, J.** (2019). *The Power of Local: How Neolocalism is Changing Business.* HarperCollins.

    - A comprehensive analysis of neolocalism and its impact on business practices, with case studies and practical examples.

3. **Harrison, L., & Morrison, T.** (2018). *Artisanal Marketing: Building Unique Brands.* Routledge.

    - Focuses on the role of artisanal products and unique branding in creating a distinctive market presence.

4. **Johnson, R.** (2021). *Community Engagement for Small Businesses.* Oxford University Press.

    - Provides strategies for effective community engagement, including local partnerships and customer involvement.

5. **Baker, M.** (2017). *The Art of Local: Crafting Authentic Experiences.* Princeton University Press.

    o Discusses the importance of authenticity in creating memorable local experiences and building customer loyalty.

Articles

1. **Williams, S.** (2023). "The Rise of Neolocalism in Marketing." *Journal of Marketing Trends*, 12(3), 45-58.

    o An article exploring the increasing trend of neolocalism and its implications for modern marketing strategies.

2. **Nguyen, H.** (2022). "Local Partnerships and Their Impact on Community Engagement." *Business and Community Journal*, 8(2), 67-78.

    o Examines the benefits of local business collaborations and partnerships for enhancing community ties.

3. **Jones, A.** (2021). "Artisanal Products: A Market Differentiator." *Retail Innovations*, 15(1), 22-34.

    - An analysis of how artisanal products can set businesses apart in competitive markets.

4. **Taylor, K.** (2020). "The Role of Humor in Brand Engagement." *Advertising Insights*, 9(4), 89-101.

    - Investigates how humor can enhance brand engagement and customer experience.

Reports

1. **Local Business Association.** (2024). *Annual Report on Community Engagement and Local Partnerships.* Local Business Association.

    - Provides data and insights on the effectiveness of community engagement practices and local business collaborations.

2. **Market Research Group.** (2023). *Trends in Local Marketing: A Comprehensive Study.* Market Research Group.

- A detailed report on current trends in local marketing, including neolocalism and its impact.

3. **Chamber of Commerce.** (2022). *The Economic Impact of Local Business Initiatives.* Chamber of Commerce.

    - Analyzes the economic benefits of local business initiatives and their contribution to community development.

Websites

1. **Local Business Marketing Institute.** (2024). "Best Practices for Neolocal Marketing." Retrieved from www.localbusinessmarketing.org

    - An online resource offering best practices and case studies on neolocal marketing.

2. **Artisan Business Network.** (2023). "The Benefits of Artisanal Products in Modern Business." Retrieved from www.artisanbusinessnetwork.com

    - A website dedicated to the benefits and strategies of incorporating artisanal products into business practices.

3. **Community Engagement Solutions.** (2022). "Effective Community Engagement Strategies." Retrieved from www.communityengagementsolutions.com

    - Provides insights and strategies for engaging with local communities and building strong customer relationships.

www.ingramcontent.com/pod-product-compliance
Lightning Source LLC
Chambersburg PA
CBHW052156220526
45471CB00004B/1699